Unleash

Your

AUTHENTIC IDENTITY

UNLOCK YOUR TRUE IDENTITY
&
PURPOSE

Dr Sylvia Forchap-Likambi

Other books by the Author:

Success Blueprint – Timeless Principles to Enable You to Identify & Accomplish True Success & Fulfilment in All Areas of Life

ISBN-13: 978-1-913266-98-1

Principles of Resolution – A Practical Step-by-Step Guide to Enable You to Identify, Set & Accomplish Your Goals

ISBN 10: 1543063780

ISBN13:9781543063783

Seven Powerful Strategies for Overcoming Life Challenges – Tested & Proven Life-Changing Keys

ISBN-13: 978-1975669584

ISBN-10: 1975669584

A Father's Tender and Compassionate Love

ISBN 10: 1479772887/ ISBN 13: 9781479772889

ISBN 10: 1479772879 ISBN/ 13: 9781479772872

TABLE OF CONTENTS

DEDICATION

This book is dedicated with love to all those seeking to unlock their true identity and unique purpose here on Earth! Enjoy the beautiful ride to self-discovery and purpose.

All my love,

Sylvia

ACKNOWLEDGEMENTS

My profound and heartfelt gratitude goes to my darling husband, Pastor Michael Likambi, for your continuous support and love towards me, ensuring that I continue to live a purposeful and fulfilled life and become all that I was created to be.

To my gracious and magnificent children and angels – Latoya, Caleb, and Baby Destiny – for enabling me to experience the exceptional joy and fulfilment that comes with motherhood, I could never have asked for any better! Thank you for making me the incredibly happy and fulfilled mum and role model/ mentor that I am today.

To my beautiful family and siblings, beloved friends, pastors, staff, colleagues, loved ones, and the millions of men and women I have been privileged to work with and serve globally—thank you for enabling me to fulfil my unique purpose of existence and continue to do so by serving you wholeheartedly with each new day I am blessed and privileged to be alive. Nothing could ever compare to the unique experience and the deep sense of satisfaction and contentment that comes from being truly authentic and living a purposeful life…

Above all, I would like to express endless gratitude and honour to my Heavenly Father and Creator, for the magnificent gift of life, purpose, and wisdom! To Him be all the Glory!

PREFACE

There's never been a more desperate and urgent need/cry than now to find our true selves, understand and distinguish what we genuinely want and need from what others and society expect from us, and get back on track to pursue our greatest and most sacred/fulfilling heart's desires. Before now, our world has never witnessed a generation of young, vibrant and dynamic men and women who seem to be so distracted, lost, and without a clear sense of identity, vision, and purpose.

With all the amazing benefits of the digital and information age also come chaos, misinformation, distraction, turbulence, and decreased productivity, if not effectively harnessed and managed. With an increasing overload of erroneous information blended with truth, it becomes more and more difficult to separate true and vital knowledge from false and trivial knowledge... Eventually, what is known, and how much of it is known (especially by our children), is almost down to the media/publicity and how viral such knowledge becomes—irrespective of whether it is true or false. Hence, there is an ever-increasing percentage of educated, yet ignorant people full of misconceptions, insularity, and without a clear sense of direction or purpose.

I am deeply touched and have so much compassion when I see great men and women and our vibrant young people with incredibly untapped and virgin potentials settle for mediocrity, or as copycats, second-class citizens, and, worst of all, in gross ignorance (due to their lack of knowledge or acquisition of misleading information/knowledge) ... despite the many free tools, resources, and, opportunities out there to enable them to become empowered, develop themselves and live life to their greatest and fullest potential! I now fully understand the famous quote that says, *"You can take a horse to the stream but can never force it to drink water."*

It is also heartbreaking to acknowledge that suicide is the leading cause of death among young people aged 20–34 years in the UK, with about three times as many men dying as a result of suicide compared to women. It is also the leading cause of death for men under 50 in the UK. The above is also true worldwide. Data from the World Health Organisation reveals that suicide occurs throughout the lifespan and is the second leading cause of death among 15–29-year-olds globally. Two years ago, it was estimated that every 40 seconds someone committed suicide, and it is projected to be every 20 seconds from 2020!

Have you ever wondered why anyone would ever reject/destroy the most precious/valuable and priceless gift of life—which is life itself? Why would someone ever take away or even think of taking away his/her own life? With the prognosis getting worse over time in spite of significant research and medical advancements, I am left to think that we must and should start looking at the root causes of this pandemic and at alternative and sustainable sources for real solutions and transformation. Could we possibly be building a suicide generation (whether deliberately or ignorantly) or a generation of young people with lost and/or misplaced identities who consequently feel worthless and unworthy to live? Why is suicide the leading cause of death among young people in the UK and the second leading cause of death among young people globally?

I strongly believe that as individuals and leaders it is our responsibility to address and resolve this tragedy before it gets out of control. As a result, there is no better time than now to get our young generation back on track. In addition, as unique individuals, it is also our ultimate chance and opportunity to shape and define or reshape and re-define our true identity, worth, values, vision, and life purpose—so we do not conform to societal norms, limitations, and expectations and hence are not misguided and/or led astray into hopelessness.

This is neither the time for us to measure ourselves against others nor to strive to be like them/perform like them or even out beat them; such an attitude in the long run disempowers us and results in a sense of dissatisfaction, frustration and lost/misplaced identity and worthlessness. On the contrary, when our focus is on becoming the very best versions of ourselves with each new day, there is no urge to compete, fit in, or please others... We become more aware of the fact that when we compare to others or compete with others, we do so in vain! We eventually become very conscious of doing the right thing and being at peace with ourselves... We stop living other people's lives, dreams, and visions; we stop trying to adapt, fit in, and/or compete—and just be our authentic selves.

The ultimate way to nurture our greatest potentials, grow, and thrive to be truly successful/fulfilled is to first and foremost identify our uniqueness, and hence our greatest potentials—and then constantly and consciously compete only with the very best version of ourselves. Only then can we be able to consciously and continually work towards maximizing our full potential/life purpose and becoming the very best superstar that we were born to become—without ever settling for mediocrity!

I am hereby urging you to invest in yourself and in your personal development and well-being and that of your children (if you are a parent) like you have never done before. Do not let this year go by without getting to know who you are, where you have come from, why you are here on this planet, what you can do, where you are going to and why. Knowing the answers to the above questions is paramount if you must live beyond the ordinary day-to-day life and strive for excellence! You must always remember that you are here for a unique purpose and were born to leave your footprints on planet Earth!

This is your opportunity to change your life once and for all and get separated from the masses... It's your time to say goodbye to mediocrity and negativity... It's your time to stop being a people pleaser and start living life to the fullest and adding value to your world. It's your time to say goodbye to old habits and relationships that do not build you or add value to your life anymore... Your time to stop prioritizing associates and people who consider you replaceable, disposable, and/ or as a mere option. You are more valuable and worthier than you could ever think or imagine — and never let anyone tell you otherwise, not even yourself!

Always remember this... Your worth and value have got absolutely nothing to do with your appearance, skin colour, race, status, class, education, background, gender, what people think or do not think about you, etc. It's all down to who you are and who you think you are. Arise, wake up, walk off mediocrity, and develop yourself today —

NOW! We aren't getting any younger with each new day. Do something today to refine your gifts, passions, talents, etc.... Please, do not step into the next year of your life any less than you got into this year or you are at the moment. If you don't grow and become better this year then, unfortunately, you will shrink... There is no such thing as staying the same because life is advancing all the time, time is passing by, people grow, things grow/expand and change, and anyone who does not grow and flow with time is automatically left behind and isolated to shrink.

Therefore, it is in your best interest to unlock your unique identity, life mission, and vision sooner rather than later in life! Of note, true fulfilment and a great life of abundance and success only come when you recognise and operate in your most authentic and unique identity and purpose—and not in another's or as society demands. On the other hand, true liberation/freedom only comes when you live your life, your dream, your vision, and your purpose.

There is only one you—a truly unique and dynamic masterpiece. Hence, there is virtually no room for fear, unhealthy competition, uncertainty, insecurity, etc. when you are your authentic self. There is absolutely no honest and fulfilled way of living life other than being true to yourself and just being who you are—nothing more and nothing less! There is tremendous power and authority that spring forth effortlessly and naturally when you live and walk in truth and in your most authentic self and purpose! This power and authority stem forth from the Divine that dwells in you and no external force or situation is capable of conquering or suppressing it.

Now, for those who may need clarity, certainty, and an in-depth understanding of themselves and why they exist, I hereby offer you this ultimate and priceless piece of manuscript to empower and enable you to gain clarity and certainty about your unique identity, and hence uncover your greatest potential/wealth and live a very fulfilled, successful, and glorious life. You must come to the awareness that success and abundance are found in every area of your life and relationships and hence are your birthright. Nonetheless, it's not sufficient to become aware of this profound and life-changing truth; you must also take the necessary steps to reach out and claim ownership of it.

In my book *Principles of Resolution*, I spoke about the importance of identifying, setting, and accomplishing our life goals so that we can live a fulfilled and purposeful life. I also threw light on seven powerful principles and laws of nature that we must apply while setting those exciting and wonderful New Year's Resolutions, which we often set at the beginning of each new year. I am sure that most of you reading this book now must have already identified and set your goals in every crucial area of your life and are currently working towards accomplishing them.

Nevertheless, I am fully aware of the fact that there will still be some people who have absolutely no idea of what they really want to achieve and, hence, are unable to set key goals in their life and there are also those who have no motivation to act on their goals and have not accomplished much yet. Never mind if you fall in one or more of the above categories... This book is purposely written and structured to enable you to identify not only your authentic identity but also what you really want in life. It is obvious that if you do not know who you are or what you want in life, you cannot have a clear vision or set definite goals. Consequently, this manuscript will enable you to identify and unleash your authentic identity, worth, and life purpose and, as a result, what you genuinely want to achieve in life that will bring you ultimate success and fulfilment. In this way, you can start planning and setting those goals so that you can have a fulfilled, meaningful, and successful life.

However, let me caution you on this; it's not going to be an easy ride... Yet, you should always remember this, you are a victor and not a victim. Whatever you may encounter during this journey, or may even be going through right now while you read this book, is not intended to break, crush, and destroy you! On the contrary, it might be necessary to break you open to reveal your true identity, full potential and worth so that you may be able to fulfil your unique purpose here. Furthermore, what you may currently perceive and consider as a mess might just be your unique message of hope and victory to the world. You've got a story to tell the world based on your experiences here on Earth giving you full ownership and authority over your story, message, and life. Whatever seem to be some stumbling blocks right now are merely stepping stones to take you higher and position you on a greater platform and altitude to be able to reach out to greater heights and to many more people than you would have otherwise been able to do without those stepping stones/blocks.

Be encouraged, knowing that I am here to hold your hands and walk with you through this powerful journey of self-discovery and transformation. I hope that today, as you read through these paragraphs, you will be greatly inspired and transformed by the renewing of your mind and thoughts.

CHAPTER ONE

WHY KNOW YOUR AUTHENTIC IDENTITY?

"When you do not know who you are or what you want in life, there is a great tendency for you to eventually settle for a mediocre life! Therefore, to live an all-fulfilling and exceptional life, it is paramount that you go back to the basics of self-identification."

Dr Sylvia Forchap-Likambi

"Fundamentally, who you truly are – your core beliefs, values, thoughts, and attitude – are grossly responsible for the way you deal with and overcome challenges in life."

Dr Sylvia Forchap-Likambi

When faced with the question, "Who are you?" what is your usual response? We live in a world where many simply do not know who they truly are or why they even exist in the first place... Identity crisis is a huge and persistent problem in our society today— resulting in so many health conditions and complications and, in some severe cases, suicide.

I know of many individuals, especially young girls and women, who cannot even stand the look of their own image in the mirror as it appears to be a complete stranger, unknown to them! In some worse cases, they profoundly detest the image of themselves they see in the mirror! Others go on living some other person's life or, even worse, the identity bestowed on them by society or peers without ever understanding who they truly are, what brings them a deep sense of fulfilment and satisfaction, and/ or why they exist.

Before we go any further on this topic, I would like us to first of all look at the definition of identity. The Oxford English Dictionary defines identity as the characteristics determining who or what a person or thing is. In a nutshell, your identity is simply those traits and qualities that define you and distinguish you from the others, hence it is very unique to you. Literally speaking, it is what sets you apart from me and everyone else on this planet. In the same way, my identity sets me apart from you and everyone out there. This is one of the key reasons why we need and/or have identity (ID) cards, such as passports, driver's licences, etc., through which we are identified and distinguished since no two people can have the same ID card.

Hence, I hereby urge you to look within; arise, wake up, step out, and identify/redefine who you are, why you exist on planet Earth, where you are heading to, and eventually stand out from the crowd! In doing so, you identify and map out your own destiny and are capable of planning for it in advance and achieving immense success and accomplishment in every area of your life and career.

You must step out and be at the forefront of identifying and redefining your authentic identity and ideal life. In essence, you must take full responsibility for your life and define/set those goals that are indispensable to enable you to become the change you want to see in your life, family, and world… You can definitely do this, if only you are willing to. You must stop waiting for people, society, situations, life circumstances, and/ or the pressures of life to define who you are, and hence determine the type of life you should live and consequently the types of goals you must set for yourself and accomplish, making it practically impossible for you to live a fulfilled and accomplished life.

As write this book, I am prompted by a burning desire within me to speak specifically to you as you read this book and stir up a great desire within you/your spirit for a new revelation of who you truly are—as a very unique and original individual. In this way, you may be able to identify, set, and accomplish your life goals and fulfil your purpose of existence.

I strongly believe that knowledge is a powerful weapon for success and victory, and I cannot emphasize this enough.

In fact, in Hosea 4:6, it says, "My people perish; my people are destroyed as a result of a lack of knowledge." However, I must place significant emphasis on the fact that knowledge of the truth is what is powerful and has the potential to bring about genuine transformation and liberation. When you know the truth about yourself – who you are; where you have come from; why you are here on this earth; what you can do; where you are going to; and why – only then can you truly start experiencing true freedom and success.

I would like to share with you a very inspiring story I read in a social media group I belong to that brings alive the power of identity. I hope this story inspires you and stirs up a burning and unquenchable desire within you to uncover your true identity and life purpose.

Here goes the story…

One hot afternoon, a hunter went to the forest and brought back an eaglet. He placed the eaglet amongst his chickens. The eaglet grew amongst the chickens and not only learned to behave like chickens but actually came to believe it was a chicken. Its chicken mentality became a mental block to it fulfilling its full potential. Instead of flying high like an eagle, the eaglet walked around like a chicken, running away from little hawks and small predators it could easily dispatch.

One day, the mother eagle came flying high looking for her lost son. When the mother eagle saw her lost son amongst the chickens, she cried out in love thinking that her now grown-up son would hear her voice and fly to meet her in the sky. But to her greatest shock and disbelief, the baby eaglet ran and hid like the chickens around it. This happened over and over again, until one day the mother eagle came when the eaglet and chickens were drinking water from a spring. When the eaglet looked at its image in the water, it realized that it looked more like the bird in the sky and not like the chickens around it. At this stage, it discovered its true identity… And this time around, when the mother eagle let out a cry, the eaglet responded; it flapped its wings and began to run … this time not away from its mother but towards her.

Now… Who are you and who do you think you are? You do not need to tell me or anyone else the answer… All that matters is that you know the answer – the truth and walk – and live in that truth and authenticity! When this becomes the case, anything or anyone unauthentic and/or impure becomes naturally separated from you—as you operate in completely different frequencies. Your old bad habits, limiting self-beliefs and associates can no longer identify with you or fit in as there is literally no longer room for such in your life.

I hereby invite you to join me on an incredibly powerful and unforgettable journey to uncover and embrace your new and most authentic self and open up to the endless new and astonishing opportunities awaiting you ... keeping in mind the indisputable fact that you are a victor—born to stand out and soar/lead like an eagle.

CHAPTER TWO

THE POWER OF KNOWLEDGE

> "Knowing others is intelligence; knowing yourself is true wisdom. Mastering others is strength; mastering yourself is true power."
>
> **Lao Tzu**

We have often heard that knowledge is power, as disclosed in the previous chapter, and this cannot be emphasised enough. As I mentioned earlier in the previous chapter, in Hosea 4:6, it says, "My people perish; my people are destroyed as a result of a lack of knowledge." Of note, knowledge is simply information. You can have information that is false or information that is true. What you should be interested in, and require for your transformation, is knowledge of the truth. In fact, Jesus said, "When you know the truth, the truth shall set you free."

What is this truth then? Does it mean we do not know the truth, which is why we are suffering or underprivileged? How come we are still living in bondage despite having countless and accessible sources of knowledge at our disposal? This is where wisdom comes into play. Hence, it is also not sufficient to have knowledge of the truth. The real transformation takes place only when you apply the knowledge of the truth acquired and in those areas of relevance in your life—which is exactly what we both need. It is, therefore, my utmost and greatest heart's desire and wish for you that you seek knowledge of the truth and, above all else, wisdom – the wisdom to be able to discern what is true from what is false, what is good from what is bad, what is correct from what is wrong, what is corrupt from what is genuine – and apply such in your life accordingly and in a timely manner in order to make it relevant and life-changing.

I guarantee you that the easiest and quickest way to keep people enslaved is to deprive them of knowledge of the truth... Therefore, you cannot afford not to know the truth about yourself and your authentic identity and worth. Becoming ignorant of this truth leaves you as an easy target and prey for exploitation and enslavement and, worst of all, a slave and prisoner of yourself—in your own mind!

For example, when we look back at the days and years of slavery, it would have probably been easy for people to be enslaved because they lacked knowledge of the truth about their identity, worth, authority, and power and were fooled into believing that they were worthless and inferior to their masters. Not fully knowing who they were would probably have made it much easier to deceive them and feed them with lies and misguided/misleading information about themselves. I would imagine that they lacked knowledge of the great and untapped potentials and resources that were entrapped within them. They probably also lacked knowledge of their inherent ability to shape and transform their lives, families, nations, and continent as a whole—and this made them conform and settle for mediocrity and even worse.

On the contrary, we could see the exact opposite amongst the blacks and Africans who had in-depth knowledge of their identity, worth, and power and would neither conform to the white supremacists'/oppressors' narratives nor the societal labels, prejudices, and racial stigmas bestowed upon them by the white supremacists and/or oppressors. The likes of the legendary Dr Martin Luther King and Nelson Mandela, amongst many others, were ready to die holding on to what they inherently believed in rather than live and give in to the popular narratives/be considered inferior, worthless, and oppressed by those who were either ignorant about their true identity, and hence full of deceit, or inherently evil and abusive.

Unfortunately, the same thing is happening in our society today, and in some cases it's taking a slightly different facet and taking place very close to our workplaces and homes. Take, for example, in today's society, far too many people, especially women, are disadvantaged, oppressed, enslaved, and constantly being exploited as objects of pleasure, abuse, etc. simply as a result of the fact that they lack knowledge of who they truly are. The vast majority of them lack knowledge of the immense potentials and abilities entrapped within them to change and shape their lives, stories, and history. They probably lack knowledge of the fact that they could change their situation and the stories they tell themselves and their children once and for all. They are unaware of the fact that they have the power to change not only their lives but also the world! In effect, women were created to nurture, nourish, lead, and make our world a much better place, and hence they have the potential and power to do so!

Most probably, when I talk of you being capable of impacting and transforming your society and the world, you are like, *"Oh come on, Sylvia, what are you talking about and what has that got to do with me? How is that even relevant in my life? I am actually struggling to make sense out of my own life and be successful and you tell me about transforming the world? How on earth can I be able to impact my nation and world?"* Guess what; I can fully and perfectly understand you and your concerns, and all of the above are very valid questions and concerns, which is the main reason why in the subsequent paragraphs I will take you through a concept and familiar setting that may be common to each and every one of us … a concept and setting that everyone is aware of, making it much more easier for you to grasp and comprehend this chapter.

Notwithstanding, you will certainly agree with me that our world is currently in great chaos, strife, and unrest, and a lot of us are unhappy about the current states of affairs in the world and also in our neighbourhoods and lives and are constantly seeking for a possible outlet or solution, while others have given up every hope and faith in a possible solution and transformation! I am of the opinion – and strongly too – that all of what we see, hear, feel, and experience in our world today is very closely linked to the fact that we have actually never known who we truly are or, even worse, do not know who we are anymore, hence we have lost touch with our true identity/purpose and the true meaning of life. We are quite ignorant of our individual and/or collective purposes of existence in this world, and, as a result, we cannot really impact our world and bring about transformation or make it any different/better than what it is today. And because we are lost and confused, we naturally and unconsciously rear and nurture a lost and confused generation of young people who are also growing without any sense of purpose and meaning in their lives and in life as a whole! What a waste of valuable resources and lives! Too often, they remain entrapped and enslaved in their own minds—battling with identity crises and insecurity.

As a result of this dilemma we now face, millions of young girls and women are constantly being abused and oppressed, simply because they or their oppressors/abusers lack knowledge of who they truly are/their intrinsic worth and hence continue to dwell in gross ignorance and their oppressors persist in abusing them. Sadly, this is also the case with a lot of blacks and minority groups in the Western world today.

I would like to take some time to specifically address every woman and/or individual reading this piece right now who finds themselves in conditions/environments where they are constantly being oppressed and abused. I yearn to speak specifically to you. I desire to stir within your spirit a new/renewed desire and zeal... A desire for a revelation of your authenticity—of your true identity as a woman and/or black, minority, etc... I want to stir a burning desire within your spirit to crave for knowledge of the truth and wisdom—now and at all times.

However, this book is for everyone who seeks to unveil their true identity and life purpose. This is the time to arise, wake up, seek knowledge and wisdom, and embark on a transformational journey to impact and transform your life, your family, your children, and your generation—once and for all. This is the time; the timing is right and just perfect ...

there is no other time like now. You can't afford to wait for other people, your parents, leaders, or even the state to come and rescue you/change your story and/or your life. Wake up, arise, and be the change you want to see in your life and in the world. You can do this! We can do this! Let's do it today—now!

CHAPTER THREE

THE DEVASTING EFFECT OF
IGNORANCE

> *"My people perish; my people are destroyed as a result of a lack of knowledge."*
>
> **Hosea 4:6**

One of my visionary friends, Dr Ben Etta, once said, "If you think knowledge is costly then try ignorance." I couldn't agree with him more. Ignorance is very costly and devastating—in fact, it's deadly! It strips us of our true power and deprives us, our children, and the next generation from reaping the benefits thereof. It is very obvious that when you do not know who you are, you will certainly never know what you really need or want in life and you will (without any doubt) eventually settle for mediocrity, accepting and validating this lifestyle as the norm. Furthermore, you will inevitably abuse/misuse yourself by not maximizing and fully exploiting the endless and great potentials that lie within you—untapped and unknown to you. Regrettably, you will also let others abuse/misuse and exploit you—consciously or unconsciously... Now, what do I mean by this?

Abuse simply comes from the fusion of two words; abnormal and use. Hence, the abnormal use of an object or an individual and/or a resource results in abuse of that object, individual and/or resource, respectively. When you abuse an individual or an object, it implies that you use that individual or object contrary to its original purpose or intent of creation/manufacture. Consequently, not having a good grasp and knowledge of your true identity, worth, and hence your purpose of existence, makes abuse/self-abuse or misuse/exploitation inevitable.

In order to bring to light the huge negative implications that are associated with a lack of knowledge (ignorance) of your true identity and what you want to achieve in life, we will now examine a few practical examples that highlight the fatal implications of ignorance. Let's imagine you are in the process of getting your driver's licence but you do not know the purpose of the traffic lights or have never seen or heard of them before. As a result, you are ignorant and unaware of the fact that when the traffic lights are green, it signifies that you can drive on, and when they are red, it signifies that you must stop.

Now, let's analyse the consequences of ignorance from the above example. If you drive on when the lights are red, two things might potentially happen: first of all, you would be accountable, liable, and fined—and you could also be convicted. The most interesting thing is that it doesn't matter whether you are aware of the purpose of the lights or not, or whether you are also aware of the law or not. Irrespective of whether you are ignorant of the purpose of the traffic lights/law or not, you will still be fined—as it is against the law to go through the traffic lights when the lights are red. Secondly, you might have an accident and destroy your own life/car as well as the lives/cars of others, simply as a result of going through the traffic lights while they are red! Therefore, ignorance is no excuse; it exempts you from neither the law nor the consequences of your actions.

Let's consider another situation where a three-month-old baby is given a mobile phone and she doesn't know the purpose or function of the phone. What do you think she will do with the phone once she gets a grab of it? I am pretty sure that the very first thing she will do is put it straight into her mouth; next, she will try to eat/bite it then maybe hit it on the floor and she will take pleasure and delight in hearing the sound the phone makes on hitting the floor. If she is left with the phone unattended, I bet she will pick it up again and will try to eat it or go through the above steps all over again until she becomes tired, bored, or distracted/attracted by something else.

In this scenario, would you say that this gorgeous little baby is mean or unkind? Absolutely no! She is probably the most gorgeous and beautiful angel that exists on this planet, and she is simply ignorant of the purpose of the mobile phone and hence will inevitably abuse and/or misuse it.

On the other hand, if I as an adult minding the gorgeous little baby do not also know the purpose of the phone, I will let her play with it (and may even join her in the game, thinking it's fun) and end up destroying it. However, since I know the purpose of the phone, I will definitely stop her from playing with it. I will not even allow her to use the phone or play with it in the first instance. This is very similar to what happens in life when we do not know the purpose of our life… Unfortunately, we let other people abuse us, and, worse still, we abuse ourselves and sadly are unaware of and unable to maximize our full potential. Furthermore, we are unable to tap into the greatness that is within us and use that to fulfil our purpose on Earth and impact/inspire others to do the same as we are unaware of/ignorant of the greatness that lies within us.

Let's consider another example, which I often use in my workshops. What do you think would happen if someone (a gentleman) walked into my office while I was having a meeting and said to me, "Hello Sylvia, great to meet you; what a handsome gentleman you are"? Am I going to get upset and become angry with him? Absolutely no! I'm just going to think that he made a mistake or might not be alright... He may even have a problem either with his sight or his mental state of being. I know perfectly well (like deep within my soul and my very existence) that I am a female. Hence, how could anyone who is normal/has good sight and is in the right frame of mind call me a man? I will initially try to correct him, by letting him know that he has mistaken me for someone else. However, if he rejects my proposition, and keeps insisting that I am a man, and continues to justify and qualify his statement, then I must leave him in his state of gross ignorance and not let it affect me or the way I feel about myself.

In all honesty, I would think he has a serious problem and needs urgent help. Hence, I will be more compassionate towards him rather than get upset with him. You will certainly meet a lot of such people during your lifetime... One time it may be about your gender, another time it may be about your race, and the next time about your hairstyle or dress or simply about the way you look or speak... There will always be something. Nonetheless, when you are truly confident in whom you are and what you represent, you don't get upset with such people in life. They are simply not worthy of your energy and/or time!

On the contrary, if I did not quite know who I am or lacked confidence in my identity, I am very sure that my attitude and response would have been quite different.

Imagine that I was male and I had just recently transformed into a woman after some surgical operations and procedures. In a situation like this, my response to the same statement from the same individual might have been quite different from that above. Following the same statement, I may start feeling very uncomfortable and thinking that something about my looks isn't quite right. I may start getting confusing and conflicting thoughts and hence perception about my true identity. I may even think, *Maybe he is right ... maybe something in me still reflects my identity as a man... Maybe the operation was not done well or maybe my face and features do not look quite feminine...* I may even start thinking of suing the surgeon/s who carried out the operation and procedures. Can you or anyone you know relate to the above? This is simply because when we do not know who we truly are, we suffer from identity crises and get all confused and sometimes upset/demoralized by people's views and opinions about us and how we look and/or act.

Now, let's look at another example that highlights another devastating effect of ignorance. This time, let's come close to our homes and examine the issue of domestic abuse. Please, permit me to make reference to this as it is one of the most common forms of abuse experienced in our world today and it is responsible for a large number of deaths worldwide and a huge drain on resources.

Of note, when I talk about domestic abuse, it could be the abuse of a male, female, and/or child. In the subsequent paragraphs, we will explore the most fundamental and common reason/s why this often happens—which in my opinion (and from my experience working with several women and a handful of men who have either been abused or are currently being abused by their spouses/ partners) is vastly as a result of lack of knowledge and/or ignorance.

As previously highlighted, we abuse an individual or an object when we use that individual or object contrary to its original purpose or intention of creation. So when you treat a child, a woman, or a man differently or contrary to the intent for which each one of them was created/ born then you are abusing them—and more often than not, it's due to gross ignorance or as a result of exploitation/oppression.

Consequently, being ignorant of your true identity and worth is detrimental to your overall well-being and how you are treated/treat yourself, just as not exploiting and maximizing your full potential gives room for others to exploit and maximize them on your behalf, to fulfil their own selfish hearts' desires, ambitions and dreams leaving you void and unfulfilled.

Of note, there are two fundamental reasons why we abuse ourselves/ others or let others abuse us. The first reason is ignorance. Ignorance of our/ their identity, worth, and, therefore, purpose will inevitably lead to abuse! The second reason is misuse of power/authority and/or exploitation. In this case, people use their free will and the power and authority conferred to them to either oppress or exploit our ignorance and/or vulnerability. The latter, unfortunately, is heartbreaking and manipulative and one of the key reasons why you cannot afford to have a misconception or be ignorant about your true identity.

You simply cannot afford to become vulnerable and easy prey for exploitation, leading to identity crisis—which has a huge negative connotation on your overall health and well-being. Having said this, is ignorance an excuse for abusing others? Absolutely no! You will still be held accountable and responsible for the consequences of an ignorant action or decision. Ignorance is deadly, it is costly, and, above all, it destroys lives—it is much more costly than the costs involved in the acquisition of knowledge.

Besides, the worst thing about being ignorant of your true identity and worth is the fact that it predisposes you not only to an abuser who lacks the knowledge of who you are/your purpose but also to self-sabotage.

Now, let's explore in more depth the issue of abuse and a possible solution to combat and overcome this. I want you to envisage an image of someone attempting to punch, kick, and/or hit you... My question to you is this: "Do you look like a ball or a punching bag?" I guess your answer is no! One thing is certain, you might not know who you are, but by virtue of the fact that you are human, you surely know some of the things that you are not. For example, it is very obvious in this case that you are not an object such as a ball or punching bag.

I know this is a very sensitive area and my profound apologies if this may stir up some pain and expose some wounds that are yet to heal. Now, please, read this and listen carefully: it is your duty and responsibility to educate and empower the abuser. However, if he/she is not interested in getting educated/knowledgeable, then there is nothing you can do about it other than let them perish as a result of ignorance and stupidity.

The most important thing is for you to know the truth about who you are and that you have the potential and power to leave that place/environment in order not to be abused, punched and/or kicked. Now, whether you choose to exercise this power and authority or not is another thing … which we won't look into at this moment.

For a woman reading this, I am fully aware of the fact that right now you may be dealing with a grown-up man at home and are wondering and asking, "But how can I stop him? How can I educate, empower or change him?" Some women may even be like, "Oh, come on, Sylvia, it's not as easy as you may think. You can't understand … you don't know what I am currently going through. If only I was a man … then it would have been much easier! As a woman, it's difficult, it's almost impossible—there are loads of challenges and limitations... Come on, don't act like you come from another planet and are not aware of this simple reality! You must be joking, but you definitely lack a sense of humour." Well, I tell you this: it is quite simple, though not very straightforward. Now, let's explore this further in the subsequent chapter of this book.

CHAPTER FOUR

UNDERSTANDING AND WALKING IN
TRUTH AND AUTHORITY

> *"Live life in such a way that your life becomes the greatest testimonial and reflection of your authority and leadership."*
>
> **Dr Sylvia Forchap-Likambi**

First of all, before I expatiate any further on this, let me reveal to you a powerful statement of truth about yourself… Your gender, race, status, or background has nothing to do with your authentic identity and worth. Hence, whether you are a Woman, Black, White, Red, Yellow, Green, or whatever complexion society has labelled you, you have absolutely no excuse—the aforementioned do not define you as a unique individual and masterpiece, and are all down to people's/society's ignorance/lack of knowledge of your true identity, worth, potential, and power.

Here I am, a brown-coloured woman (I love to say brown rather than black because if we were going by colours, this is the colour of my skin), wife, and mother of three amazing children, and a true testimonial of the authority and conviction with which I write and communicate this life-transforming and fundamental principle to you ... and if I can be this confident and secure in my identity – being fully aware and confident of the fact that who I am is not defined by my gender, marital status, and/or the colour of my skin, hair, eyes, etc. – then guess what; you can do exactly the same—whatever your gender, status, skin colour, or eye colour.

However, if you don't know who you are or you see yourself as disadvantaged, inferior, a less worthy being or a failure, you may never be able to comprehend and unlock this powerful truth and transformational tool and pass it down to your children and the next generation of leaders. Hence, my ultimate goal is to inspire and empower you through this book to unlock your greatness and unleash your true identity so that you may be able to impact the next generation of men, women, children, and leaders ... and leave a lasting legacy.

Hence, if you think being a woman makes you disadvantaged, then be reassured by the fact that every single human on the planet has been conceived and brought forth into this world by a woman, and there is no perfect human on Earth—not one! If there is anyone living on planet Earth today who is not born of a woman and/or is perfect, please get in touch with me and challenge me on this. You might be asking, "But what has this got to do with putting an end to the violence and abuse I encounter at home and leaving a legacy?"

My response to the above question is very simple, yet profound. As a woman, you are more powerful and influential than you could ever think or imagine ... with an inherent advantage over men. Now, let me simplify and break this down before you start cringing. Now woman, this question is for you. Are you aware of the fact that from the moment of conception the precious little foetus (baby) in your womb can hear you? What does this mean? It simply means that you have the potential and power to start impacting this precious little unborn life within you right from conception. You may not be able to change them when they are grown-up men, but you have the potential and power to shape and mould them when they are unborn and still young so they can develop and grow up into respectful, caring, and loving gentlemen.

As a mother, you must learn to speak powerful words and prophesies into your child's life, even when he/she is only a tiny little foetus. Speak to your unborn child/children. Tell them they're wonderful; tell them they're powerful; tell them they're beautiful; tell them they're unique and tell them they are the best children in the entire universe—the best children that have ever existed on this planet!

Impact them through the power of your words and positive affirmations. Impact your daughters and sons alike while they are still in your womb and unborn. Why not shower them with love and powerful affirmations that will build and shape their fundamental beliefs about themselves and life? Constantly tell them who they are and how great and marvellous they are. Such words will eventually form the foundation of their beliefs and the knowledge they have about themselves when they eventually grow up. It will definitely form part of what they will turn out to believe in and reflect to their spouses and the world. Consequently, you can greatly impact grown-up men and women when they are still your young sons and daughters ... and even better ... when they are yet unborn!

For example, I have two beautiful and incredible daughters aged 14 and five years, respectively, and I tell my elder daughter all the time, "Sweetheart, you're the best daughter and girl on Earth; you're very special, unique, and beautiful just as you are—let no one on the face of the earth ever tell you otherwise, not even your parents or your teachers— nobody! You are born for a purpose and everything about you and the way you look is designed to fulfil that unique purpose. You are a victor and not a victim, a leader and not a follower." I also constantly speak the same words of praise and positive affirmations to her five-year-old baby sister (my little angel and gorgeous princess).

On the other hand, this is what I often say to my son — who is now 11 years old: "You are the best boy and son in the entire world; you are a great and intelligent young boy and you are a victor and a superstar! You are destined for greatness and success! You are very strong and powerful and these qualities and traits are bestowed on you by the Divine to protect yourself, your sisters, your friends, and the weak/most vulnerable of society." Hence, we can start telling our children (sons and daughters) all these powerful words and affirmations at a very tender age.

As mothers, it is our responsibility and duty to tell our sons that they are strong in order to protect and not to hurt the weak. We must teach them and constantly tell them never to abuse or raise their hands and/or voice to a lady as true gentlemen don't do this, just as true ladies do not do this either. When we start educating and empowering this generation of young and vibrant boys from birth and while they are still very young, we then have the potential in this way to change an entire generation. This is so because when your son grows up, having heard your voice over and over constantly telling him, "You are strong to protect the weak... You are strong to protect yourself and every single girl and woman in the world... You dare not abuse, insult, or hurt a lady," he will eventually grow into a great man who protects and nurtures, and not otherwise. Eventually, he will pass on the same teachings to his own sons—acting as an authentic and perfect role model for them and their children's children. The same also applies to our daughters, who will grow up to be great and confident women, mothers, and role models— teaching their sons the same. In this way, we shape and build the next generation of children, families, and leaders.

It is well acknowledged that when we empower and transform a single woman, we empower and transform an entire family, generation, nation, and the world at large. In addition, there have been several studies and much research highlighting and/or justifying the unique role of women in leadership and the immense success of many businesses/organisations led by women or with women in senior leadership positions. A study in 2019 by Jack Zenger, CEO of Zenger/Folkman, a leadership development consultancy, and Joseph Folkman, president of Zenger/Folkman, showed that "Women Score Higher Than Men in Most Leadership Skills." Their latest research studies in 2020 demonstrated that "Women Are Better Leaders During a Crisis."

The above and other studies simply highlight the significant leadership qualities/ skills and authority that women process as a whole.

CHAPTER FIVE

THE POWER OF SELF-AWARENESS

> *"The beginning of every transformation in life starts with self-awareness."*
>
> **Dr Sylvia Forchap-Likambi**

The beginning of any transformation in life starts with self-awareness. Self-awareness is the most powerful and greatest tool you need to bring about genuine transformation. The first area of awareness that is needed is awareness of who is going to actually undergo and accomplish this journey and transformation, which in this case is you. Self-awareness leads to self-confidence, which is profound trust and belief in yourself. You could never believe in someone you do not trust and you could never fully trust someone you know nothing or very little about.

As a result, if you don't know who you are, there is an absolute tendency (it is actually a fact) for you never ever to be able to trust yourself, hence you will not be able to believe in yourself. Self-awareness begins with a deep sense of awareness of who and where you genuinely are at this stage of your life and who/where you would love to be, and a need for change.

In the subsequent paragraphs, I will be providing you with a series of examples that will help you in your quest for your true self/identity. These simple and very practical examples will be able to help you to become aware of how you perceive yourself at the moment and how you would love to be perceived and identified both by yourself and others moving on.

In your journey of self-awareness, it is first and foremost important that you become aware of the indisputable truth that you are human and that every single human on the planet is imperfect. There is no perfect human being in the world, and, sometimes, what you may perceive as your shortcomings or weaknesses are not necessarily shortcomings/weaknesses but simply an indication of that which you were not born to accomplish and which is therefore unrelated to your purpose.

For example, the main function of the eye is to bring sight to the entire body and, consequently, its greatest strength. For this reason, the eye is naturally equipped with lenses and all that is required to enable it to function to its maximum potential and bring light and sight to the body.

However, if you were not aware of the purpose and function of the eyes, you could easily be made to think and believe that the reason why eyes cannot breathe or talk is because they have a defect or weakness. Notwithstanding, the eyes were never designed to breathe or talk, so this could never be a weakness of the eyes. In the same manner, you are naturally equipped from conception (via your unique DNA) with everything you need to fulfil your unique mission and purpose here on the earth.

Secondly, you must become aware of this fundamental truth and be convicted in your spirit that all humans are born equal and every individual is unique and endowed with great abilities and potential to impact our world, regardless of their gender, skin colour, religion, status, and/or the circumstances surrounding them. There is no one superior or inferior to another—not even one!

Take, for example, if we examine the different parts of our body; none is greater or inferior to another, yet they are completely different with very distinct roles and functions. For instance, your eyes and your nose are two distinct parts of your body with two different roles and purposes. Your eyes are not superior to your nose because they can see while your nose cannot see ... nor is your nose inferior to your eyes as a result of its inability to see.

On the other hand, because your nose can breathe while your eyes cannot, it does not make it any better or superior to your eyes and vice versa... They all work together in harmony for the edification of your entire body. In this case, your eyes' main purpose is that of sight, and you can see me and everything around you because you are using your eyes and maximizing their potential to fulfil their purpose. You cannot close your eyes then use your nose and expect that you are going to be able to see me and everyone/everything else around you. However, if you were the eyes but did not know that the main function or purpose of the eyes is to see and to bring light to your entire body, and someone comes in and starts insulting you, trying to put you down and degrade you, based on your inability to breathe like the nose then you may start thinking you aren't good enough or are inferior when compared to the nose — based on your inability to perform like it!

Now let's imagine that at the instant or the moment when you were insulted and degraded for not being able to breathe you were surrounded by a bunch of "nose friends" who are all able to breathe and do so with great ease too! However, because you are certain about your identity as an eye and the very purpose for which you are placed on the body – which is for sight – you can confidently ignore every insult thrown at you in an attempt to demoralize you or make you feel inferior and less valuable. You instantly become aware of how ignorant the abusers are and simply educate them that you cannot and were never designed and placed on the body to breathe but to see and bring light to the entire body. You might as well just remind them that you are unique and different from the nose—an eye.

However, this is where the problem and crises begin. If you don't know that you are an eye, and hence lack knowledge of the purpose of an eye, you could think that something is genuinely wrong with you … and this negative thought could be further amplified by simply looking around you and clearly seeing that all your "nose friends" around you are breathing and even the mouth is sometimes capable of breathing and also doing something else such as eating, which you are unable to do as an eye! You may start dwelling in self-doubt and even start asking questions like, *How come all the other parts of the body can do a variety of things that I as an eye cannot do?* You then start getting confused and doubting yourself and your ability to succeed even more. You eventually lose all confidence because you think that you cannot breathe, you cannot eat, and you are also unable to speak!

But when you know that you are meant to see, when you know that your purpose is to give sight to the body, it does not matter what any other person says. You are going to tell them that you are not meant to breathe, you are not meant to eat; on the contrary, you are meant to bring light to the body.

You become convicted that if there is ever a problem where your body cannot see then there is a problem with you (the eyes) and you can then go to work on yourself to restore your eyes/sight back to its optimal state—where it will be able to function and serve to its full potential. Now, something is wrong with the eyes, which has resulted in a subsequent weakness that inhibits your ability to function to your full potential as an eye and needs restoration. Consequently, when you know who you are and your purpose, you are better placed and equipped to understand that some perceived weaknesses of yours are not really weaknesses but simply an indication of all that which is not your purpose or meant to be in your life ... and therefore all that you are not and were never destined to do and/or become—just like the eye, whose inability to breathe is not a weakness but an indication of what it is not meant to do. On the contrary, the eyes are equipped with all that is needed to make them function perfectly to bring light and give sight to the entire body. In the same manner, you are naturally equipped at creation/conception with everything you need to be identified and equipped with to fulfil your purpose on here on Earth.

Consequently, you need to start asking yourself simple but profound life questions like what are your greatest strengths. What are the things you can do so well and enjoy doing with great ease without actually struggling? Once you become aware of whom you are, your strengths and your purpose, it doesn't matter what any other person thinks or says about you… You become very confident.

On the other hand, when we don't know our strengths, purpose, and who we truly are, and people tell us otherwise, we get very upset, hurt, and let their words affect our emotional and mental state and overall well-being.

In the subsequent chapters of this book, we will be looking at some very fundamental and vital questions you must ask yourself and respond to in order to help you identify who you truly are, and hence your purpose of existence.

CHAPTER SIX

WHO ARE YOU?

> *"Unless you know who you truly are as an individual, you get lost in society, trying to identify yourself with some group, community, tribe, gender, race, culture, religion, class all of which take you further away from your true self and the incredibly unique individual that you are."*
>
> **Dr Sylvia Forchap-Likambi**

Now, who are you? To appropriately respond to this priceless and timeless question, it would be very helpful for you to know that prior to your birth and existence your identity had already been established and subsequently concealed within your genetic code (DNA) and spirit being. Humanly speaking, your DNA actually has some very unique and specific codes within it, yet to be decoded, and is largely (if not fully) responsible for those unique traits and characteristics that distinguish you and set you apart from others. Overall, it is responsible for providing an indication of who you are and will eventually become. Of note, not even a child has the same DNA as the mother; neither do identical twins—even though we call them "identical twins."

Notwithstanding, you have a very crucial role to play to ensure the correct decoding of your DNA so that you may become all that you were created and destined to become. To accomplish this, you must first of all see and acknowledge yourself as the great individual that you are destined to become and not as who you are at the moment or based on your environment and background. The desires and vision you have for who and what you are destined to become must guide and drive your every motive and action in life henceforth until they become rooted and engraved in you to form your fundamental beliefs, values, and way of thinking—given that your unique identity and who you are stem forth from some of the very profound and fundamental beliefs you hold about yourself and life, which then shape your values and way of thinking and, eventually, over time, are made manifest or reflected in your words, actions, and habits. In fact, from your actions and habits, your destiny could be predicted. You don't need a prophet or some sort of a magician to tell you how your life will go. This could be established by simply taking a look at the manner in which you consistently act, which will eventually define and determine your habits.

Therefore, it is paramount that you become aware of your foundational beliefs, values, and thoughts and re-evaluate, analyse, and reshape them accordingly. The latter are tied to your destiny and the individual you will eventually become… For as a man thinks, so he is.

Therefore, the above question has got nothing to do with your qualifications, current financial/economic status, background, gender, race, and/or current condition. For instance, I won't expect you to respond to the above question simply by saying, "I am a doctor," or, "I am a lawyer." Absolutely no! Being a doctor, a lawyer, or an engineer does not really define who you truly are. This is so because these are simply achievements and you existed even before the qualifications were gained, and for this reason your identity precedes your current achievements and/or economic and social status.

Take, for example, whenever there is a job advert in search of a doctor, lawyer, or an engineer, it is very obvious that in order to even qualify to apply for such jobs and be considered and shortlisted for an interview, everyone who applies for the position must either be a doctor, a lawyer, or an engineer, based on the specific role they are applying for. However, what happens after applying for the role and being fully aware of the fact that only one candidate is required for this role? You must remember that everyone applying is a doctor, a lawyer or an engineer, based on the specific role they are applying for. Now, tell me, what will set you apart from the other fully qualified doctors, lawyers or engineers like you who also applied for the specific role? What will make you and not them the ideal candidate for the job? Why would the potential employer prefer one doctor over another, one lawyer over another one, or one engineer over another? In a nutshell, why should they prefer you to the others who applied for the same position with exactly the same qualifications—assuming some of them even graduated with distinction while you did not?

Of note, there are some very crucial characteristics and attributes that shape and define you and hence set you apart from the others. There are some core qualities that only you alone possess. So who you truly are would be defined by your core beliefs/convictions, values, your attitude/way of thinking, speaking and/or doing things, and also by some of those vital habits and passions of yours.

I want you to take some time and reflect profoundly on this question: WHO AM I? In your response to the question, write down as much as you can. In addition to this, you should write down your strengths, your passions, and your vision. Try to find out more about those great and unique strengths and talents/gifts that you have that may easily and readily set you apart from the masses.

25 Fundamental Questions to Help You Identify Who You Are

By clearly responding to the questions below you will be able to have an in-depth knowledge of yourself and about what really matters to you and brings you joy and fulfilment.

1. Who are you? How do you identify yourself?

_____
_____
_____
_____
_____

2. Where have you come from? What is unique about your origin and background?

_____
_____
_____
_____
_____.

3. Why are you here? Why do you exist on planet Earth?

_____
_____
_____
_____
_____

4. What are the fundamental beliefs you hold about yourself, and why?

_____
_____
_____
_____
_____

5. What are your core values? What are the principles that you will never compromise on?

_____

_____

_____

_____

_____

6. What are the things that excite you most in life? What are you most passionate about in life?

_____

_____

_____

_____

_____

7. What types of activities or work bring you fulfilment and satisfaction?

_____

_____

_____

_____

_____

8. What does being successful mean to you? When will you be able to confidently say that you are successful?

_____

_____

_____

_____

_____

9. What is your purpose for living/why are you alive and not dead?

_____
_____
_____
_____
_____

10. What are your greatest strengths?

_____
_____
_____
_____
_____

11. What are your greatest weaknesses?

_____
_____
_____
_____
_____

12. What is your long-term vision? Where do you see yourself (and what are you doing) in the next 15–25 years from now?

_____
_____
_____
_____
_____

13. What can you do? What skills, gifts and talents do you
have that you can readily use today and at this stage of
your life?

_____
_____
_____
_____
_____

14. How would your friends or parents describe you?
Friends:

_____
_____
_____
_____
_____

Parents:

_____
_____
_____
_____
_____

Do you agree with their descriptions?

_____
_____
_____
_____
_____

Why or why not?

_____
_____
_____
_____
_____

15. List two situations or scenarios in which you were most comfortable and relaxed.

_____
_____
_____
_____
_____

What specific components were present that made you feel that way?

_____
_____
_____
_____
_____

16. What types of activities did you enjoy doing when you were a child?

_____
_____
_____
_____
_____

What about now?

_____
_____
_____
_____

17. What motivates you?

_____
_____
_____
_____

Why?

_____
_____
_____
_____

18. What are your dreams for the future?

_____
_____
_____
_____

19. What do you fear most in your life?

_____
_____
_____
_____

Why?

_____

_____

_____

_____

_____

20. What stresses you most in life?

_____

_____

_____

_____

_____

What is your usual response to stress or life challenges?

_____

_____

_____

_____

_____

Do they make you more resilient or more fragile?

_____

_____

_____

_____

_____

Do they make you bitterer or more compassionate towards others, life and/or yourself?

_____

_____

_____

_____

_____

21. What qualities do you like to see and appreciate in other people?

_____
_____
_____
_____
_____

22. Do you have many family members and friends with these qualities you just described above? Why or why not?

_____
_____
_____
_____
_____

23. What upsets you and makes you angry the most in life?

_____
_____
_____
_____
_____

24. What is your natural response to what makes you angry? What do you do about the situation?

_____
_____
_____
_____
_____

Unleash Your Authentic Identity

25. What relaxes and calms you down?

_____

_____

_____

_____

_____

Why?

_____

_____

_____

_____

Take as much time as you need to go through these questions and come up with definite answers. Find a quiet and peaceful place to sit down and relax when you go through these questions and avoid any form of distraction and/or interruption. Such a setting will give you the unique opportunity to delve deep within you and search inwardly for some of those hidden answers and qualities that lie within. Reflect on each and every question before attempting to respond. If in any doubt, speak to loved ones and your parents who know you very well. You may even seek a life coach or mentor (if you do not already have one) to support you throughout this unique journey to unleash your most authentic identity and purpose.

51

Why Are You Here?

At this point, we can now move on to explore and respond to the next soul-searching question, which is: **Why am I here?** Why are you on this planet? Why did you come here and not go elsewhere? Your being here is purposeful and simply not by chance or trial. As Mark Twain put it, there are two most important days in your life—the day you were born and the day you find out why. On the day you were born, you come into existence as a legal human on this planet, while on the day you discover why you were born you start living and experiencing the true meaning of life. It is the day you eventually discover the purpose of your existence, and on this day you stop existing and you start living a life of greatness, a life of purpose, and a life of fulfilment and true meaning. It's like you have been dead all this while and you have just been born again or have resurrected to live again. When you discover the reason for your existence, you stop living a mediocre life and go on to live a life of excellence—because you were actually born to thrive and to excel. Hence, it is crucial that you find out why you are here on planet Earth. You are no chance; you are no mistake because you are here for a specific purpose. Actually, you could never live a fulfilled life if you didn't know who you truly are and the purpose of your existence.

Start searching deeper, look into your strengths again, and maybe take it even further by singling out the greatest strength/s amongst your strengths. What are your greatest strengths? What do you do with great ease? All of these questions will play a significant role in guiding you towards identifying your true identity and purpose.

What Can You Do?

The next question you may have to consider asking yourself in order to gain more insight and clarity, which also goes hand in hand and/or is interconnected with your strengths, is what can I do? Having ascertained why you are on this planet in the first place, the next and most reasonable question to ask and answer is what can you do while you're here? The fact is you were never just placed here to find out why we are here (our purpose) and then celebrate... Hurray! I found my purpose... Great! Once purpose is discovered, the next step is obviously making it become a reality—by fulfilling it through your actions and daily habits/lifestyle! And what you can do is again linked to your strengths... You would not be expected to accomplish a task for which you are not equipped with the necessary resources, tools, knowledge, and/or skills! For example, even the best medical doctors in the world when assembled in an empty clinic without a single piece of equipment or medication could never be able to function to their full potential and ability... Hence, your creator will never hold you accountable or responsible for a battle He never equated and assigned you to fight. In other words, you will never be expected to fulfil a purpose that you have not been equipped and wired to fulfil. Hence, our strengths are one of those fundamental pillars that define what we can do. Another pivotal pillar is your passion/s! What are you passionate about? Some of us may have stopped focusing on or talking about our passions because of our current situations, our circumstances; please go back to those passions because these are also linked to some of the things you were created to do and enjoy doing. In effect, your key drive for doing them is not for financial reward, praise, pleasing others or even to prove something! Your key drive is the fulfilment, satisfaction, etc. that come from living that passion of yours. Fulfilment is a divine signal within you to affirm purpose/the execution of purpose.

After looking at why you are here, what you can do, and your passion/s, what next? It's not enough to just sit back, relax, and do these things... You are heading somewhere—in essence, you are doing the above mentioned things with an end goal or result in mind ... be it success, accomplishment, victory, etc.

What Is Your Vision?

Where Are You Heading To? It's very obvious that wherever you are on the planet right now and reading this book, you are actually in the present. But after this day what next? After the next day what next? Where is your journey leading you to? Where are you going to? What is your destination? What is the great plan? Examine this question in greater depth. Visualise your future... What does it look like? How does it feel? Where do you want to be or would rather be to be genuinely happy, at peace, and fulfilled? Another question you should be asking yourself is, "What will I do when I get there?" It's simply not enough to get there. For example, so many people go to university but go for different/diverse reasons. Some are teachers, some are professors, some are students, some are cleaners, some are trainees, etc. So what will you do when you get to that final destination? Why are you going there and not somewhere else? Why would you have this vision and not another? All of the above are critical questions to be addressed which will take you closer to your purpose. Finally, once you've gone there, you know why you're there, and you're now working towards fulfilling the latter, a final and conclusive question you must ask and seek to genuinely respond to is this... How does it feel?

How Does It Feel Living Your Vision?

How will you feel when you finally get to that final destination of your journey and you are now doing all the things you went there to accomplish? What does finishing the race/journey mean to you? What's the ultimate price that awaits you at the end of this journey? What does success mean to you and feel like? If your answers to this last question (which is all about the way you feel) create fulfilment, satisfaction, inner peace, and that "Wow" effect, then this is really where you were born to be and what you were born to accomplish—your purpose! If your responses are like, "I'm going to feel really great; I'm going to feel powerful and amazing; I'm going to feel fulfilled; I am going to feel accomplished and successful; I am going to feel incredibly awesome," then go for it! This is actually who you were born to be and in becoming that person, you have not only found your authentic identity, but you have also fulfilled your ultimate purpose of living.

In addition, this is where you were born and destined to be and what you were born to be doing when you get to that destination. As a result, by the time you eventually exit this planet, you will be holding nothing back and will leave a lasting legacy behind. In other words, you must have fulfilled your maximum potential, benefited your children, your generation/humanity, and have left a legacy.

Of note, success is not necessarily about amassing riches and all of the material stuff around us... We know of so many whom society has defined as successful/rich people, who have unfortunately felt empty, void, worthless, and eventually taken away their own lives by committing suicide. It is therefore very evident that success is not about amassing riches, but rather, it is about knowing who you are – your purpose – because that is the essence of real fulfilment and success.

As I come to the end of this chapter, I would urge you to start working on your unique journey to find out who you truly are – your purpose of existence – and go out and live the wonderful, beautiful, and exceptional life that you were born to live and deserve to live and make those goals and vision of yours a tangible reality.

The next chapter will take you to the core and foundation of your unique identity and solidify everything we have discussed until now. Now let's move on to explore and unveil the heart and soul of your identity and uniqueness, which I have reserved until now.

CHAPTER SEVEN

WHAT IS YOUR SOURCE?

> *"Once you know where you have come from (in other words, your source) you have a better understanding of what you are destined to become."*
>
> **Dr Sylvia Forchap-Likambi**

We have all come from somewhere and that origin is linked to our source and most authentic being. This is so because in our source lies our identification and hence our uniqueness and diversity. We did not just come into existence following the waving of some magical wand or magical explosion. Besides, when you have a sense of belonging, rooted in your source, it gives you a sense of assurance and security.

Hence, my million-dollar question to you is this: "Where have you come from?" I am very aware of the fact that someone currently reading this book is probably an orphan whose parents have passed on and therefore he/she may not have a close family relative or carer to look up to. But the truth and reality is we are all unique products of conception from the fertilization of our biological mother's egg by the sperms of our biological father (irrespective of whether they are currently with us/known to us or not). Furthermore, I believe in an even greater source and higher power than the mortal and physical bodies of our biological parents—the Divine and Almighty God, our Creator. Hence, we all have a greater source ... including orphans.

Before I proceed any further, let me make this very clear... I'm not a religious minister, but whether you believe or not in the former statement it's not my role to convince you through this manuscript, but rather my intent is to give you the unique opportunity to explore this further and deep within your soul and spirit... To seek, unravel, and know the truth and live it fully and authentically so that you do not perish because of the lack of knowledge or as a result of ignorance and/or the rejection of knowledge of the truth.

The truth is there is a greater source beyond the physical and knowing and acknowledging this truth is in your favour and for your own benefit. It will only do you well and not evil if you understand where you come from. For example, understanding that you come from someone far greater than any living being on Earth, who is a Creator, will enable you to walk in authority and power, knowing full well that you are connected to the source and the supply of all things ... and have direct access to abundance too. You become aware of the fact that HIS DNA runs in you (just like your earthly parents' DNA) and hence His Spirit is in you and dwells in you. Consequently, believing in this simple yet profound truth is all for your benefit. It's like getting to know that you are a son or the daughter of the queen of England. What difference will this finding make in your life? Ponder…

Once you know where you have come from (in other words, your source) you have a better understanding of what you are destined to become. In essence, your source or origin plays a huge and critical role in defining your identity and life purpose. Take, for example, an orange seed; though similar to a lemon seed, once it is told that it originates from an orange fruit it immediately knows its identity and has a sense of unshakable confidence in itself and all that it is destined to become once sown and nurtured. It becomes confident in its ability to grow and produce oranges and only oranges based on its source—knowing full well that it was extracted from an orange fruit and not from a lemon fruit! You might have heard this before: "By their fruit you will recognize them." Mat 7:16

Consequently, the final orange fruit is established within an orange seed long before it becomes a fruit. To put it this way, whatever seed originates from an orange fruit has the potential to produce oranges. Hence, every orange seed is excited and confident in fulfilling its purpose of growing into an orange tree and eventually producing oranges … irrespective of the delay in sowing it.

Let's take another example. If you look at an orange fruit, a lemon fruit, and a grapefruit, they are quite different from each other; however, the seeds of these three fruits – orange, lemon, and grapefruit – all look so alike... When placed together, you cannot quite distinguish which of these three seeds will grow up to become an orange tree/bear oranges or which of them will grow up to become a grapefruit tree/bear grapefruits or a lemon tree/bear lemons, can you? Absolutely no! You may not be able to identify or recognise the fundamental differences in these three seeds, yet they are significantly different with distinctive intrinsic qualities, traits and characteristics unique to each one of them. For instance, all that is needed by that grapefruit seed to produce grapefruits and nothing else is encoded within its seeds. However, people might see these three seeds and immediately think that they are all the same and originate from the same fruit due to their similarities. Notwithstanding, they are fundamentally and intrinsically different and from three distinct origins!

Likewise, no one can know you by just looking at your background, your external features, skin tone, and/or current circumstances. No one can claim to know you or predict your destiny based on who and what you have become as a result of your current situation or circumstances in life because the greatness within you, which is called your potential, is entrapped within you, in your unique DNA (and yet to be decoded and unravelled), and no one can translate or interpret that just yet—except your Creator (because He actually designed you from creation and entrusted you with that unique DNA that will eventually unfold to reveal everything about you and your destiny, hence you were a finished product even before you were born).

I will give this final example before I move on. I am very aware of the fact that in the previous chapters I placed much emphasis on women and their seeming "super powers". Now I would like to take some time to acknowledge and give honour to men.

Men are equally and distinctively unique and wonderful. In fact, my first book is entitled *A Father's Tender and Compassionate Love* and explicitly describes the incredibly compassionate and unconditional love and guidance offered to me by my wonderful earthly father and heavenly Father. While writing this book, I was profoundly struck by the discovery I made while reading a variety of literature and research studies on fathers, some of which I will share here with you in the subsequent paragraphs.

I uncovered that in Aramaic father means "source" ... provider. When I got this revelation, I thought to myself, *Hold on a minute... What does this mean? How could men be the source? We all know that it is the mother who conceives... She is the one who becomes pregnant, nurtures, and brings forth the child to the world, etc. Hence, how could we even begin to think that*

63

men could be the source? Nonetheless, as I pondered profoundly on the question of source and searched further for a deeper meaning and revelation of the above questions, it became decisively clear and evident to me. After significant reflection, I eventually realised that it did make a lot of sense though.

Let's take a step back to evaluate and analyse the significant role/s fathers play in the conception and birth of their children, so as to better understand why a father is referred to as the source. Now, let's explore this together. Let's begin by looking at a woman's menstrual cycle. Each month, a woman ovulates and releases an egg, which, if not fertilised by a male sperm to produce a foetus, is eventually discarded through her menstrual cycle for that month. Hence, a woman's egg/s would never be able to give birth to any life without the sperms of a man (conception), and consequently it will be discarded as a dead body in her menstrual cycle. Consequently, if left unfertilized, the female egg disintegrates and the uterine lining is shed during her period. We know full well that a woman's egg is discarded every month during her menstrual cycle—it's not even considered as blood that is important for the body as it doesn't serve the body.

On the other hand, when the biological source, the originator of the human life, the sperms of a man, comes into contact with that same egg and penetrates it, what we call conception takes place within the egg of a woman and a new life is formed. Hence, this is the origin of a new being. We need to actually recognise and celebrate men as well for their indispensable role in the conception and birth of every human life.

In fact, research and various psychological studies have shown that most of the problems we face today in our world are highly correlated to the absence of fathers in the homes. For example, in the United States of America about 90% of all young male offenders in prison come from absent-father homes.

In 1993, research by Hill O'Neill revealed that youths who never had a father living with them have the highest incarceration rates (they come from homes without fatherly figures/role models for the young men) while youths in father-only households display no difference in the rate of incarceration from that of children coming from two-parent households (Harper and McLanahan, 2004). Studies by Coley and Medeiros in 2007 revealed that the more opportunities a child has to interact with his/her biological father the less likely he/she is to commit a crime or get involved with the juvenile justice system.

For the female inmates, a study by Snell, Tracy, & Morton in 1991 revealed that more than half of them came from a father-absent home. It is also evidenced that females with an absent fatherly figure at home have lower self-esteem and confidence issues when compared to young girls growing up in homes with both parents or in a single father home.

A study by Davidson A in 1990 also demonstrated that a high percentage of gang members come from father-absent homes and attributed this to a possible need for a sense of belonging... It may be a case where the gang leader may fill the role of father, often leading members to model his negative behaviours. In 2012, the above evidence was confirmed by Leving, who demonstrated that having a father in the child's life greatly reduces the likelihood of a child joining a gang.

In 2004, Bronte-Tinkew et al. further demonstrated that children who come from father-absent homes are at a greater risk for using illicit substances at a younger age. On another note, in 2002, a study by Hoffmann demonstrated that children who grow up in a home where there is no father figure/a father is absent are at a greater risk for abusing alcohol and other drugs. In another study by Mandara & Murray, 2006, in which researchers examined the impact of father absence on African American boys, the findings revealed that the boys who came from a home without a father presence were more likely to use drugs than boys who came from a home where a father was present, concluding that the involvement of a father in a child's life can therefore be a protective factor against child and adolescent substance use.

In addition, numerous studies have also shown that coming from a fatherless home can also negatively impact a child's mental and emotional health and well-being, leading to significant mental health problems, such as anxiety and depression. In 2007, studies by Flouri demonstrated that children from a father-absent home are more likely to become depressed, have suicidal thoughts, anxiety, social withdrawals, and school absences if they see or hear their parents fighting. Fatherless children may develop thoughts of worthlessness when they compare themselves to other children who have fathers and wonder why their father abandoned them. This may also lead to an increased risk of suicide and/or self-injurious behaviours.

All of the above evidence is not to say that all children who are raised in a father-absent home will experience adverse outcomes ... absolutely no! Some of these children will be outstanding and excel in every area of life... This is not to define or sentence a child to a definite destiny... Nonetheless, with this said, available evidence cannot be ignored. The importance of our source in shaping and defining our identity and destiny and providing us with a definite sense of belonging is not to be undermined in anyway.

In the UK, the Office of National Statistics (ONS) revealed that in 2009 nine out of ten single-parent homes in the UK were headed by women. Where have the men gone? It is, therefore, very important for us to recognize and acknowledge the significant roles fathers play in their children's lives and families. It is critical that men/fathers understand their roles in the family and society and come back home. We need them in the family—they are a critical part of a functional and stable family unit and society. We need to know and acknowledge how central/pivotal their presence and involvement in their children's lives are. No matter how great a woman is, her son needs a male figure and role model to look up to … something a woman/mother could never become or offer her son. I have been married now for 15 years and I have three amazing children (two daughters and a son). I am definitely a wonderful mum and I love my children so profoundly. Notwithstanding, there is only so much I can offer to them as a woman and mother. There is just something about their father's presence in their lives … it brings some sort of assurance, order, and much more … and this is further evidenced by the countless studies and research outlined above.

For those children who have not been privileged to grow up with a father figure or who have not had a wonderful and role model father in their lives, this book is not intended to make you feel uncomfortable or inadequate—far from it! I am also not accentuating a feeling of loss, guilt, and grief... This is by no means written to make you feel less worthy in any way or like you've lost a significant part of your life and should dwell in feelings of sorrow, regret and/or grief either. On the contrary, it is intended to revive and reignite a new and glorious beginning for you... A rebirth! You can still thrive in life and successfully become all that you were ever created to become, living a life of purpose and fulfilment, even without a father figure in your life. I would like to take this unique occasion to remind you that we have all come from a greater source … a powerful and higher being. With or without a physical father presence in our lives, we have definitely originated from a well-defined and unchangeable source/origin. Now let's look beyond our family...

There is a greater Father who designed the masterpiece and unique creation that we each are even before we were conceived and born/came into existence. To me that Almighty Father is God Almighty. I don't know whether you believe in Him or not; in any case, I am not going to dwell on this. However, like I said before, knowledge is power (or more correctly potential power) and knowledge of the truth is actually more powerful and brings about liberation and true freedom. So, whether or not we believe in the existence of God or are simply ignorant about His existence does not change the fact that He does exist.

On the other hand, becoming aware of the fact that we have a greater source gives us a sense of belonging and security. When you definitely know where you come from, you then know your source/foundation and roots and it becomes very obvious that when trials and challenges come your way, you will not be shaken and will remain rooted in your foundation. We literally become like a home built upon a solid foundation, which is not blown away by every wind or storm that blows on it. In the same manner, a tree that is profoundly rooted with its roots expanding deep within the soil or the ground can hardly be uprooted no matter what storms blow on/against it... It could be shaken but it cannot be uprooted. Leaves may fall off, and branches too, yet it will not be uprooted. But if we have a tree with shallow roots that are not well grounded, it is obvious that the least wind/storm will uproot it... Life's trials, obstacles, and challenges are similar to those winds/storms blowing against the house or tree. This is evidenced in the several positive outcomes experienced by children growing up in a home with a father (source) present who provides a solid/unshakable foundation and protective shield from external/negative factors and/or environmental influences.

CHAPTER EIGHT

IDENTITY BIRTHS CONFIDENCE

> *"Knowing who you are is the foundation and gateway to unwavering confidence."*
> **Dr Sylvia Forchap-Likambi**

In this chapter, I will take some time to talk about myself. People often ask me, "Sylvia, what is the secret behind your immense confidence?" "You're a very confident lady," they usually add. Most people I have worked with have asked me the above question at one point of my career or another. Some associate it with/give credit to my educational background and career success! Nevertheless, I always respond with a smile, saying it has absolutely nothing to do with the latter, but, rather, it has all to do with having an in-depth and unwavering knowledge of who I am and where I have come from—my unique identity, worth, and, hence, life purpose. I always remind loved ones, colleagues, and my students/mentees of this simple truth: who we truly are is not defined by our qualifications and/or titles.

Let's take a look at the above philosophy in more detail and throw more light on why I am very confident. First of all, as highlighted above, it comes down to knowledge, a comprehensive knowledge and understanding of who I am – my identity – which further reveals my worth, value, and life purpose.

Like I mentioned before in the earlier chapters of this book, knowing, for example, that I am an eye and not a nose is to know that my greatest strength/purpose is to give sight/bring light to my entire body. Hence, whenever there is a problem with my sight, and my body can no longer see, then I know I have to actually work on my eyes and the underlying negative/pathological condition/s that have impacted its ability to see so as to be able to restore sight/light to my entire body.

As a child growing up in the beautiful nation of Cameroon, in the west of Africa, where I was born, I was always a very confident little girl. Looking back to my childhood, I now realise that my dad played a very significant role in building my confidence... In effect, I think it's only fair to say that I owe almost all of my confidence to my wonderful dad, which is one of the reasons why I wrote the book *A Father's Tender and Compassionate Love*. My mum was equally a very loving and caring mum, who expressed so much love and care towards me and my siblings as well. Even though mum and dad are both of late today, nevertheless their light and love still dwell in me... I do know for sure that their legacy lives on in me and I am an authentic product of their unconditional love and care, which is why you could probably benefit from my life and work today.

My dad was an amazing and incredible father who taught me so much in life and empowered me to unlock my authentic identity, self-worth, and value and to never settle for any less. He profoundly believed in me, which translated into me believing in myself in return. Mum also profoundly believed in me, which further boosted my confidence.

Of note, confidence is simply trust ... a profound and unwavering belief/trust in someone or in something; while self-confidence simply means trust in the self. You can barely be confident when you don't know or trust the person or thing you are expected to have confidence in.

Hence, it would be very difficult for you to trust yourself, and subsequently develop unwavering self-confidence, if you do not know yourself very well, and you couldn't comfortably, confidently rely on yourself/ your judgements and/or decisions. Simply put, you can't have confidence in someone or something you do not know or know nothing about (and this includes yourself). The more you know about yourself, someone, or something the more you can trust yourself, that person and/or thing, hence the more confident you are.

Don't get me wrong; we can still trust someone we have never met or known before and are meeting for the first time. Let's consider a common scenario ... trusting a pilot that we know nothing about and are meeting for the very first time we are about to board a plane and fly—and this happens each time we are flying! Even though we do not know the pilot, still we entrust our lives and those of our loved ones into their hands as we make the decision to fly with them. Why? How come my above statement does not apply here?

Despite not knowing the pilot, one thing we know for sure and which makes us confidently board that plane is this: every pilot responsible for flying a plane has learned extensively how to pilot a plane and is qualified to do so. We also know that no pilot who has not learned extensively to fly a plane will be allowed or permitted to do so, thereby putting the lives of countless passengers at risk. Hence, we trust the airlines, aviation companies, and/ or the rules and regulations that govern the aviation industry, which is why we will sometimes choose and trust certain airlines over others, despite them being more costly. Some people have vowed never to fly with certain airlines/aviation companies due to their lack of trust in them (which stems forth from the knowledge they hold or have read about them), irrespective of how exceptional some of their pilots may be.

Having said that, let me now take this opportunity to share with you some of the fundamental truths I know about myself/my identity that gives me a tremendous sense of self-confidence and that may help you develop an unwavering confidence in yourself too. I will start from the very basics; I am fully aware of the fact that I am human, which implies that I am imperfect... Absolutely imperfect! I am also very conscious of the fact that I have some great strengths and weaknesses too, and I fully and totally embrace my weaknesses while acknowledging and celebrating my amazing strengths at the same time. Most importantly, I focus on my unique strengths, as they define me and set me apart, not my weaknesses... One of which is my inherent ability to speak from the soul and, inspire, uplift, and teach others. I have a natural gift for connecting with others and speaking straight from the heart.

I am fully aware of the fact that my strengths are far more important than any weaknesses I may have because my strengths are those qualities and traits that clearly define me and set me apart from others. They are those distinctive qualities that will determine the things I can do exceedingly well while I am on this planet and hence enable me fulfil my purpose. I generally do not focus on my weaknesses, yet there are some weaknesses that may actually hinder me from becoming the best individual that I was created and destined to become, and I continually work on such weaknesses to develop and enhance them—such that they don't get in the way of my strengths and hold me back from fulfilling my maximum potential and life purpose.

At the tender age of seven, I was very confident and had a clear mental image of who I wanted to become and where I wanted to live when I grew up. I knew exactly (almost exactly) what I wanted in life. I wanted to become a medical doctor. Specifically, I wanted to become a gynaecologist. While growing up, there was a very successful and devoted gynaecologist in my neighbourhood who inspired me a great deal. I admired him so much so that I also wanted to become a successful and outstanding gynaecologist. Furthermore, I wanted to study in Italy because the said gynaecologist also studied in Italy. Despite knowing nothing about how I would get there or finance my studies, I was determined to study there and was very confident that, when that time came, I was actually going to study in Italy. My long-term goal was to eventually settle in the UK with my family because I did not want to settle in a non-English speaking country, since I am an Anglophone Cameroonian.

It was my greatest and somewhat only heart's desire to study for my doctorate degree in Italy … and eventually settle in the United Kingdom. This was my dream, and I was confident I could achieve it…

In addition, I have always been a naturally curious child, intrigued and fascinated by the human body and how it functions to keep us alive and heal us when we get unwell. In fact, my dad used to call me (the smallest amongst my siblings then) his *pocket lawyer…* I guess I could only be a "pocket lawyer" then given how small I was. Interestingly, my mum also called me her *"attorney general"*. You could instantly tell that this little child was no ordinary run-of-the-mill *"African child"* and there was something bigger in her. There was a seed of greatness in her and growing up in such a nurturing and loving environment greatly contributed to nourishing and nurturing that seed of greatness in me.

Nonetheless, as the youngest of five siblings and still attending primary school at the time, I had quite a journey to undertake and, to say the least, a great deal of "last born" hindrances to overcome. Did any of the above really matter to me or preoccupy me? Absolutely no! For example, the fact that by the time I got to university my beloved and hardworking parents must have spent a huge fortune on the education and welfare of my elder siblings didn't really make much difference to me and to my ability to dream beyond my wildest imaginations. What seemed to be the reality NEVER conditioned the capacity/magnitude of my dreams and heart's desires…

All I ever knew and thought of was becoming a gynaecologist and studying in Italy, with the intention of later settling in an English-speaking nation—specifically, England. In effect, I strongly believed that whatever I could conceive and believe in my mind I could undoubtedly achieve. I knew with great certainty that wherever there is a will there will definitely be a way—sooner or later.

As mentioned earlier, the only reason I chose Italy as my number 1 and only choice for university was that one of the most renowned gynaecologists in my city (who was my friend's dad and resided in my neighbourhood) earned his medical degree in Italy. I was greatly inspired by him and I immediately thought that in order to become an exceptional gynaecologist like he was, it was vital to study in Italy since that is where he studied! Never mind the fact that I was a seven-year-old girl! I was convinced that Italy was the best place to study medicine in the world—it was the real deal!

Consequently, I was determined to get and become the very best from Italy, and nothing else really mattered! Did I think of the cost implications? Absolutely no! Did I think of my elder siblings having to go to university before me, hence putting considerable burden on our parents' finances and resources? Absolutely no! Did I think about what my dad, mum, siblings, and even relatives thought about this? Absolutely no! Did I seek anyone's approval or opinion on this decision of mine? Absolutely no! All I knew was the fact that this was my dream and my dream alone, and I was responsible for making it become a reality... PERIOD. An audacious seven-year-old, right? No wonder Dad called me his "pocket lawyer" and Mum called me her "attorney general"!

I had a very unique and exceptional childhood and upbringing; I am truly blessed and privileged to have come from the family and home that I come from. I never lacked anything growing up as a child, and I strongly believe that much is expected of the one to whom much has been given. I also attended some of the best boarding schools in my country and my dad made me believe immensely in myself and in my ability to thrive and succeed in every and any given situation and environment. He made me believe I was a very special and gifted young girl with so much to offer to the world, and he believed I could achieve whatever dreams and visions I had. Both Mum and Dad knew that I had so much potential within me and they both believed in me. They taught me most if not all of the foundational values and ethics I have today, which grossly shaped me into becoming who I am today.

Dad and Mum brought me up to know and acknowledge that there is an Almighty Creator, a heavenly Father and God. Dad, especially, taught me a lot about Him and profoundly believed in Him. He ensured that we went to church every Sunday and on all special occasions and reminded me very often that I am beautifully and wonderfully made and destined for greatness and success and that it didn't really matter what others thought or said about me, God's definition and description of me was final. These powerful words and declarations formed the bedrock of my belief system and unwavering confidence.

I grew up to become a confident and courageous young girl with an unwavering faith, which became the core of who I am and the fundamental beliefs/core convictions I hold to this day as I write this book and share with you some of these deep truths. I came to the understanding that I am truly unique and special and that it's perfectly okay for me to make mistakes and all that really matters is correcting those mistakes and drawing from the experiences and lessons learnt. I became comfortable with making mistakes in order to learn or to fall so I may be able to rise up again... To me, every fall or mistake was a priceless opportunity to learn and gain more knowledge and wisdom in the areas where I failed or did not excel so I could become better and more effective with each new day I am blessed to live. In addition to the above, I never compete with anyone or ever try to be like another person. I am committed to always being myself and staying true to who I am, no matter what. The truth is I could never become another person, just like no one could ever become me. I am an original and a masterpiece, and so too are you, and it is my greatest heart's desire to channel this message to you through this manuscript so that you thrive and excel in all you do and become.

Now, let's fast-forward and see what became of that little confident seven-year-old girl who knew exactly what she wanted in life. Thirteen years have gone by so quickly, and I have just finished my A-level exams with an outstanding result. I am now ready to get into the world of university but, most importantly, into a completely strange land and foreign nation where English wasn't even the first language—my Italy! Did everything go as smoothly as I had dreamt and envisaged? Not at all, but I will focus on the most gigantic mountain and barrier I was yet to encounter and overcome, hence highlighting my unshakable beliefs and confidence!

It was finally time for me to move to the capital of Cameroon, Yaoundé, to live with my eldest sister and study the Italian Language Course in the Italian Embassy, amongst other things. What a great six months I had studying the language weekly and getting acquainted with my new lifestyle. It was now four months into the course and everything was going so well. I was already fluent in Italian and, as always, I was one of the best students in my class! You see, I never get into anything I love with the intention of being anything less than the best! Neither do I go in with the intention of competing with others… I simply go in with one goal and one purpose only—to be and give my very best and only that! Most probably, others don't come in with this intention and that's why I almost always end up being the best ☺.

It was now time to write that famous and qualifying Italian Language Exam, which would determine and set apart those students who were ready and destined to fulfil their dreams and ambitions in Italy from the masses who had also been studying the language but would need to think of alternative options and dreams as their Italian dreams gradually faded away... Well, the confident Sylvia is never a stranger to exams and knew she was definitely destined for Italy to fulfil her long-term dream of becoming a gynaecologist! But guess what; I can't even believe I am writing this! Oh well... The marking system that year had changed and a higher pass mark (well above average) was established in an attempt to allow fewer students from Cameroon to further their studies in Italy, I guess... It sounds like a pretty good excuse...

The results are finally out ... and guess what; no one in my class made it—not even me! We were told that apparently only one anglophone student in the entire nation made it beyond the higher qualifying threshold mark! Of note, this student lives in the French Cameroon region and also studied in the French education system... Notwithstanding, he is very intelligent and would never fail any exam! You may be asking, "But what has being anglophone or francophone got to do with this, Sylvia?" Now, let me explain; the fact that Italian is a "Neo-Latin" language, and so too is French, makes it easier for French-speaking nationals or "francophones" to learn/understand/speak the language—hence the outstanding results from our francophone peers. On the contrary, English is not a Neo-Latin language, which makes it a bit harder, yet possible, for English nationals or "anglophones" like my friends and me to study/ understand/speak the language! I am by no means trying to make an excuse for our average/unsuccessful results as such a barrier simply means that we have to work twice, thrice, or even 10x as hard … and why not?

I was thinking, *Is this the end of my Italian dream? Am I going to be the very one to sabotage my own dreams and ambitions?* I pondered. I am not the type to fail an exam for whatever reason; I am not the type to easily give up in the face of a "failure" or "mountain". My sister was heartbroken and disappointed to see my 13-year dream suddenly come to an end or so she thought… *I am never going to deliver a message of failure to my dad or mum. I have never been a failure and I am not ready to become one now.* I thought. They had never known me to ever fail an exam that was based on merit, hard work, intelligence, you name it … and I was not ready to introduce this new concept to them just yet! I was thinking, *Dad has made a huge sacrifice to ensure I finally go and*

further my studies in Italy, and I am not ready just yet to be the
one to blow all of this up—No Way!

I was about to carry out one of the most unrealistic and courageous acts that would change the life course for many anglophone Cameroonians including me! I told my sister I was going to call the ambassador's home and speak with him. Of note, I was not asking for her consent; neither was I asking for her opinion on this. I was simply giving her notice, and being polite of course, since I was to use her landline to make the call!

I vividly remember picking up the telephone directory and searching for the Italian ambassador to Cameroon's residential telephone number, which I got! My rationale for not even attempting to call the Italian Embassy was to bypass the many obstacles and barriers I would have encountered to get to him. Calling the embassy would mean having to go through the secretary, cultural attaché', and many more people before getting to him (if at all I was fortunate enough to get to him), something I had no intention of doing!

I then embarked on my next phase—CALLING THE AMBASSADOR! I remember picking up the phone and confidently dialling the ambassador's number! How could I ever forget this very crucial and decisive moment? I was sitting there relaxed and ready to share my concerns as the phone rang… Then, suddenly, "Hallo," a lady's voice echoed from the other end of the phone.

"Hallo," I responded.

Behold, it was the ambassador's wife and this was my moment! I introduced myself to her in Italian, trying my best to sound mature. We engaged in a good six or seven-minute conversation, maybe even longer in "undiluted" Italian. She was amazed by my fluent Italian and remarked, "But you speak Italian very well, how come you did not pass the exam?" This was my final chance to resolve the crisis we were faced with or regret my entire life!

I then explained in fluent Italian how the change in the scoring system had left many anglophones, including me, very disadvantaged, despite knowing and speaking the language very well. I also told her that I was amongst the best students in my class but none of us made it! I made her to understand that the purpose of my call was to request another chance for us all from her husband, the ambassador; another test, in whatever format they desired, including an oral test where we would be able to prove how fluent we were in Italian! She was absolutely lovely and very empathetic and compassionate too! She immediately requested that I write a letter expressing my concerns and a proposal, addressing it to the ambassador, and take it personally to the embassy—where the ambassador would be expecting it. I then expressed my heartfelt gratitude to her and wished her a good night.

Now I was super excited and immediately reached for the phone again to call my other friends (who were also amongst the best in my class) and arrange a meeting the next day! I also called our Italian teacher, Sister Paula, who absolutely loved us and was very disappointed with the outcome of the exam results; remember, we were her brightest students but didn't make it! I asked if she could endorse a letter written by my friends and me (we were four in number), which she happily and instantly agreed to! Besides, she requested that we met with her once we had drafted the letter. We wasted no time in getting this done the next day and going over to see her with the draft. She read it, was impressed, and endorsed it, backing it up with a statement confirming that we were the very best of her class and some of the best students she had ever worked with. How I wish I had kept a copy of this letter!

Finally, it was time to take the weighty letter to the embassy and deliver it as requested. Within a week of handing in that powerful letter, an official communication was made over the radio calling all Cameroonian anglophones from the entire nation who took the exam in different regions of the country that year but didn't succeed (even though they scored above average) for a second chance! Yes, a second chance! An oral exam! This had never happened in the country's history! Yet, that isolated and unrealistic/unreasonable, courageous, and purpose-driven phone call changed the nation's history forever! Everyone involved from the entire nation was summoned to the Italian Embassy in the nation's capital for the first Italian oral exam ever! This day forever changed the life course of many … many who were once declined were now accepted and set to travel to Italy to fulfil their ambitions and dreams, including me of course. Except for my three friends and me, none of them knew what actually happened behind the scenes that led to this fateful day that changed their lives forever … and maybe they're finding out for the very first time as they read this manuscript!

Never change your vision, lose confidence in yourself or lower the bar because of life circumstances as there will be many in your lifetime. On the contrary, believe in yourself, re-strategize and stay focused on your dreams and vision. The only real limitation to what we can achieve or become is our mind, in the beliefs we cultivate and hold about ourselves.

Though initially wanting to become a gynaecologist at a tender age, as I grew older and became more mature and conscious of the various medical disciplines, I then changed my mind about this. The reason was simple; I became intrigued by medical science, and our body, wanting to know more about how our body works, with a key interest in our blood cells. I came to the realization that becoming a physician or a medical doctor would mean becoming a specialist who could administer already known drugs (regardless of their side effects and/or efficacy) to cure diseases that are already known/diagnosed. In other words, I would need to use available medications for pathological conditions that were already known and existing, regardless of their side effects and/or limitations. Nonetheless, I wanted to know and do more... I wanted to be able to discover new diseases that had not yet been identified and be able to develop new therapeutic tools and pathways to cure existing illnesses/pathological conditions that were yet to be uncovered, understood, and diagnosed.

As a very inquisitive and curious child who was always asking questions about almost everything and anything, most of which ended up without satisfactory answers, I immediately understood that I had a lot of work to do in order to satisfy my curiosity and insatiable quest for knowledge and also get more compelling answers to my questions. I needed to research more, know more, and discover more... As a result, I deviated from my initial vision of becoming an outstanding gynaecologist and went on to study pharmacy— finishing with a Doctor of Pharmacy degree from the University of Ferrara, Italy. My rationale was to first and foremost understand how drugs work and how they are formed and excreted out of the body with the hope that someday I would be able to find a cure for some of those diseases or ailments for which at the time there were no remedies or clinical treatments. This was my inspiration and drive for getting into the pharmaceutical field and, eventually, into medical research. With an in-depth knowledge of drugs, medical research would enable me to identify new prognostic and diagnostic tools/factors.

I then went on to earn my PhD in Italy (with a special focus on leukaemia, a type of blood cancer), during which time I also studied in Sydney, Australia, as part of my PhD program. At the end of my PhD, I then worked in Italy for a year, after which I was ready to move on and fulfil my childhood dream/vision of settling in the UK. This meant I only applied for jobs in the UK and was successfully offered two different jobs in two different hospitals and cities. To me, it didn't matter where I came from or what skin tone/colour and gender I had. Of note, when I applied for these jobs, no one knew me in these hospitals, nor did I know anyone. I also applied as a Cameroonian citizen, which meant that if I was offered any of the jobs, I would need to get a working permit and visa to be able to migrate to the UK and take up the position. Furthermore, while I travelled to the UK for my interviews, all logistics such as travel expenses (ranging from flights to train tickets and taxi fares), hotel accommodations, and meals were fully catered for by the employers, even though I was yet to be interviewed and considered for the jobs.

Once I was offered the jobs and made my decision about which one to accept, I then had to apply for a working visa from the British Embassy in Rome, Italy. As part of the application process, a series of documents was required, which included a working permit issued by my new British employer and a letter explaining why an African (a non-European citizen) was offered the role when there are a lot of British and European citizens with similar qualifications and experiences. In a nutshell, they wanted to know whether the employers had considered and exhausted all their options of offering the job to their British and neighbouring European citizens without success before finally offering the opportunity to an African (me in this case)! In response to this requisite, I received the letter and my work permit from my new British employer to support my application. In this letter it was emphasised that amongst all of the candidates interviewed (I think 38 or so, I can't quite remember the exact number now) for the position, I was the best candidate with the right set of skills, qualities, expertise, and experiences that best met the specifications they needed for the job. In other words, it was never about race, nationality, background, and/or gender but about the unique traits and qualities of their ideal candidate, which I fully met.

So, why am I telling you this story? How relevant is it? When you know who you are, you stand tall; you are confident; you believe in yourself whether others believe in you or not; you set the example; you set the pace because you so much believe in yourself; you walk confidently and people notice that there is something very unique about you and the way you present yourself and they are attracted to you, irrespective of your race, gender, and/or background. Some may even ask, "What is it about this man?" "What is it about this woman?" and they eventually start to believe in you because you demonstrate this trait consistently in everything you do. Hence, knowing who you are births unwavering confidence that makes you courageous and fearless and opens up endless doors and opportunities/possibilities for you.

CHAPTER NINE

DECODING YOUR UNIQUE
FINGERPRINTS AND IDENTITY

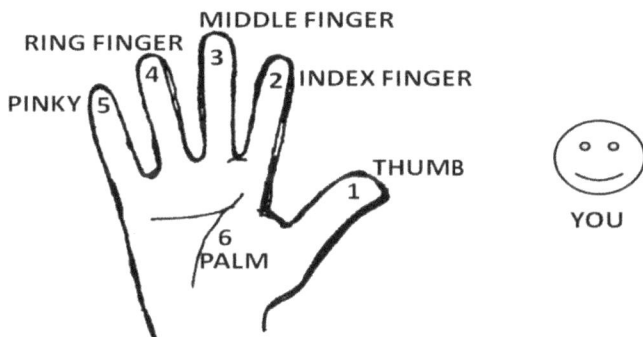

The Palm Identity Model

The palm identity model is a unique model and simple activity/demonstration I came up with and often use during my workshops and mastermind programs on "Unlocking Your Authentic Identity". It is based on my own philosophy and interpretation to simplify and elucidate the subject of identity and purpose. Now, this may as well summarise this entire book. And if there is anything you will not forget and constantly have a vivid image and interpretation of, I believe it will be this model/exercise.

In this chapter, I would like us to explore this model and undertake the associated palm exercise. Wherever you are right now, I would like you to sit down in a comfortable seat in an environment with no distractions or interruptions. When you are comfortably seated or even lying down, I want you to raise your right or left hand up—either hand is okay and suitable for the exercise. Place your chosen hand vertically in front of you at eye level (with your fingers close to one another and pointing upwards). For example, if you are doing the exercise using your right hand, your palm will be on your left and the back of your hand on the right. See image below.

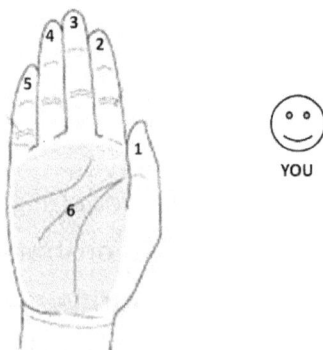

Keep your hand upright in this position as you respond to the following questions:

Looking at your hand and fingers, what can you see? Precisely, which fingers can you see?

Write down all the fingers you can see, starting from the one closest to you, and give each finger a number from one to five. Then, by each finger, write down a word or two to describe how clearly and fully or how much of that particular finger you can see while your hand is comfortably positioned in front of you and in between your eyes. Ensure that you are not straining your eyes and are relaxed. Write down your answers below.

....

....

....

....

....

....

....

....

....

....

....

....

....

....

....

....

....

....

Now let's go through this together. I will assist you with this exercise. Take note of the following observations/interpretations, which form the basis of the palm model and exercise.

1. The first finger you will see is your thumb—you can see your entire thumb very clearly, without any obstructions. Of note, whilst your thumb is directly in front of you, it is also the shortest of all five fingers. I want you to label this **PAST.**

2. The next finger you see is your index/first finger— almost entirely and very clearly too. I want you to label this **PRESENT.**

3. The third and subsequent finger you can see is your middle finger. Of note, a significant part of this finger is covered by your index finger and is unseen. Yet, you can see the tip clearly. It is also the tallest of all your fingers—hopefully ☺ (for most people). I want you to label this **BELIEFS/CORE CONVICTIONS.**

4. The fourth finger next to your middle finger is your ring finger—though you may not be able to see this finger at all from your current position, you are still aware of the fact that it is there, next to your middle finger, and you can also feel it. I want you to label this **PASSION.**

5. The fifth and tiniest finger, which is next to your ring finger, though you may not be able to see it at all, is your pinky finger. Just like the ring finger, you are aware of the fact that it is right there, next to your ring finger, and you can also feel it, though you're unable to see it from your current position. I want you to label this **VISION.**

6. Another very evident and obvious part you may not physically see from this position, but which is present, is your palm—it keeps your fingers connected. I want you to label this **ATTITUDE.**

Of note, what keeps all your fingers physically "connected" and intact/upright is your palm (this is literally speaking and not scientifically) and it is necessary for the understanding, interpretation, and effectiveness of my palm model. Let's imagine that you were to physically cut off your palm and remove it from your hand (something you would definitely never do and should never ever attempt to); what will be the outcome or effect? Your fingers will definitely fall off and apart from each other in no particular order. If so many hands were to undergo this process with the fingers all detached and lying on the floor haphazardly, some people may not even be able to identify which fingers belonged to them and which were not theirs, especially in a situation where we had many other similar fingers on the floor.

DECODING YOUR FINGERPRINTS

Now, after labelling each finger from 1 to 5 and the palm and writing down what you can comfortably see and/or perceive, I want you to go a step further, this time with your imagination and the interpretations I will provide henceforth:

1) YOUR PAST:

Let's imagine that your thumb represents your past. Hence, Thumb = Past (the code for your thumb is your past).

Remember, you can see your thumb clearly; it is right in front of you, uncovered and revealed. Your past has already happened, it is fully known to you and to all those who know about your past or knew you then. It's very clear and evident and you do not need any prophet or magician to tell you what your past would look like as it has already manifested.

In cases where you may have very shallow knowledge of your past or might have completely forgotten the details and significant events of your past or do not know your past very well, or have forgotten a huge part of it for whatever reasons, there will always be people around you who know your past well and all you need to do is reach out to them and ask... In fact, some have made it their business to constantly remind you and/or show you your past and even hold on to it, especially the negative and depressing parts/narratives. So your past is well known and evident. Your parents might also tell you more about your past, just in case you might have forgotten. Furthermore, it might have been a horrible/traumatic or sad past and an experience that you would rather forget, block, or even delete from your memory.

Regardless of all that has been said or done to you in the past, I want you to know that it does not define you and change is possible and inevitable. You may even say, "But yes, they are right ... all they said about me is true." Okay, remember this... You are only human and to err is human. Do you remember from the previous chapters what being human means? It literally means that you are imperfect and have a series of weaknesses besides your strengths. It also means that you will inevitably encounter some setbacks and "failures" in life/make some mistakes from which you will learn and grow.

Consequently, if you have ever been told that you are a failure then that is okay too... No big deal. I've got weaknesses/ limitations too, but I am here to remind you that my weaknesses do not and will never define me or shape me into becoming who I am. My strengths, on the other hand, determine that. I want you to write the following questions down on a piece of paper, addressing yourself:

• Who am I?

• Why do I believe/think I am this person I just described above?

• Who told me this narrative about myself/my identity?

Evaluate your responses and clearly state from where your identity stems forth. If they are made up of mostly the negative narratives you have been told in the past, then I want you to start writing down a new narrative, and hence the identity that you would love to have and share with others. Even though our past plays a significant role in shaping the course/direction of our lives, and therefore destiny, it isn't fully responsible for whom we become. Unfortunately, for many people, their past plays a huge role and is solely responsible for how they see, identify, and present themselves now and in the years to come. Such people are locked in their past and have become victims of their past.

Examples of some of the narratives that you can write down, so that you can overcome and defeat the negative self-talk/chatter and limiting beliefs once and for all include:

- I am human.

- I am imperfect.

- I am perfectly imperfect – for a unique and Divine purpose.

- I'm born and destined for greatness.

- I am successful – success is my birthright.

- I can achieve all that I desire to achieve.

- Whatever my hopes and dreams are, I can certainly achieve them.

- My past does not define me – my vision/ purpose does.

Never allow people to define you by your past. Do not let people or society put you into a box or box you into your past. Do not allow your past or statistics to define or predict your future. Do not let people judge or label you because of your past… Or even better, SAY NO to all manner of labels that are beneath greatness, success and your vision.

If there is anything you need to know about yourself, then you have to go back to your origin and your source to find out who you are. Your origin and source precede your past. Hence, you are much more than what you or others see in the external. You are much more than that situation you went through in the past or you are currently going through.

2) YOUR PRESENT:

Now let's imagine that your second (index) finger represents your present. Hence, Index finger = Present (the code for your index finger is your present). You can see this full well; like your past, your present is evident... It is the now—your current life and reality. Nevertheless, the narratives must be told by you. It is very obvious that you know your present because you're living in the present right now. Maybe you are thriving; you are doing extremely well; your business is successful. Maybe you are suffering; maybe you are being oppressed; maybe you are depressed. Whatever the case, that is what you see and live in the moment.

However, just like your past, your present reality or circumstances/condition does not define you and never will—unless you consciously or unconsciously allow it to. It is only temporal ... and by tomorrow all that which is today will once more become a thing of the past with the same rule and principles that applied to the thumb/ past! You are much more than that challenge you are going through right now. All of the things that we see are subject to change. However, the intangible things we do not see are eternal and unchangeable—trapped within your DNA and spirit.

Remember your present circumstance/status is not your identity. Your current job and/or title are not your identity and do not define you. Your present condition and circumstances do not and will never define you. The current state of your health and well-being do not define you either.

Never allow people to define you by your present circumstances/condition. Do not let people or society put you into a box or box you into your present condition. Do not allow your current health, educational, and/or financial status to define or predict your future. Do not let people judge or label you because of who you are today or the type of job you are doing today... Once again, SAY NO to all manner of labels and definitions that are beneath greatness, success, and your vision.

3) YOUR CORE BELIEFS

Let's imagine that your middle finger represents your core beliefs/convictions. Hence, Middle finger = Core beliefs (the code for your middle finger is your core beliefs).

Look at the middle finger; you can see the top. It is the tallest finger of all your fingers, although most of it is hidden and covered by your index finger, which is your present life. Consequently, you can't see most of your middle finger. This finger represents your core beliefs/convictions. It represents those core beliefs you hold that will in turn shape your values and hence attitude in life. They are the unique qualities and characteristics that hold you upright and confident and guide you to fulfil your purpose/succeed in life. On the other hand, if these core beliefs are not strong enough and very unstable/shallow, then they become a significant barrier/obstacle, holding you back as a prisoner of your past/present life circumstances and inhibiting you from living beyond your past/present and fulfilling your heart's greatest desires/maximum potential and life purpose. Hence, they are either responsible for your rise to greatness or your fall and defeat. They are those core beliefs you hold about yourself (past, present, future, and identity) that make you become confident. They are the foundational pillars upon which your life and success are built. Just as you cannot see the foundation of a home or the roots of a tree, as they are within the ground, so too you cannot see the majority of this middle finger from your current view or position. Nonetheless, the foundation of a home or roots of a tree are the key determining factors in how solid that home or tree will become and how much they could withstand a great storm and/or wind and not be blown away or uprooted respectively.

This finger literally represents who you are. It actually shapes and defines who you become. They are responsible for developing those qualities that are engrained within you. They govern those qualities that are hidden but keep you grounded, tall, confident and unshakable/unwavering at all times. They determine how resilient and persistent you become. In order for you to hold any beliefs that do not reflect your past or present life circumstances, you must be able to see beyond your past and present circumstances... In other words, you must overcome the past and current hurdles/obstacles that are in front of you, obstructing you from seeing who you truly are (and represented by your thumb and index finger), which is shaped by your core foundational beliefs/convictions.

You must be able to break down the barriers of your past and present in order to access and build your life on the foundational pillars/beliefs and values that you hold. For example, by bending your thumb and index fingers, you are able to see a significant part of your middle finger and not just the tip. With such exposure/awareness, you are now in a position to better understand yourself and the reason why you see your past and present and interpret them the way you do... Because your narratives and the way you see and present yourself are not determined by your past and present experiences but by your perception and hence interpretation of these. For example, two people can go through exactly the same situation/experiences in life and yet their interpretation/narratives of the experiences are very different and, in some cases, very contrasting.

Consequently, your past and current life experiences are not necessarily responsible for whom you become, but your perception, understanding, and interpretation of such experiences are. On the other hand, your past and present do not determine the direction/path of your life but your core beliefs/values and the lessons drawn from your past and present. This may also represent what your parents, loved ones/friends, trusted sources, acquaintances and/or society have told you in the past/about your past and present condition ... and you believed their narratives and are unconsciously holding on to these limiting beliefs that have shaped your fundamental beliefs about who you are without your being fully aware of this fact.

For example, if all your parents ever told you while you were growing up were words that crushed you and made you feel worthless, such as, "You are not good enough; you are horrible; you are a loser and a failure," etc., then you may grow up believing that this is genuinely who you are based on your past experiences and unconsciously see and describe yourself accordingly.

Let's assume that, at the moment, you are encountering some difficult life challenges and your past has been horrible/traumatic; actually, there is a stigma attached to you as a result of your horrible past. Your present is also horrible as a result of your past and you continue to hold on to this stigma from the past with you—everywhere you go. Guess what I am about to tell you; your core convictions/beliefs play the ultimate role in defining you and your current reality—not your horrific past and/or present challenges/trauma. If only you can still belief that you are born to thrive, you are a great and amazing individual who is destined for success and greatness, then you can still succeed amidst all odds. Your convictions and beliefs will actually determine who you become and seal the verdict. It is the bedrock of your being. You can change those limiting and destructive beliefs you hold about yourself and your life right here and now. You can rebuild your foundation, if what you currently have is a shaky and weak foundation. You can start cultivating those uplifting and empowering beliefs and do away with all the disempowering, destructive, and limiting beliefs you currently hold about yourself/your identity.

You must stand firm when it comes to those core convictions and beliefs that you hold and never compromise on them. Look at someone like Dr. Martin Luther King, who fought so hard for what he believed in and refused to give up on his core convictions about every human being born equal. He was not ready to compromise, even to the point where it cost him his life. Nelson Mandela was willing and ready to go to prison rather than give up on his core beliefs/convictions about equality and freedom for all. He spent a significant part of his life in prison fighting for what he strongly believed in. Hence, you must not let anyone oppress/devalue you because of your core beliefs. You must fight and stand for what you believe in. It is more noble and fulfilling to die fighting for what you strongly believe in/have strong convictions about than live life without any foundational beliefs to hold on to and, as a result, compromise on your core beliefs/values and follow the masses with beliefs and values that are contrary to yours and that you do not believe in.

Hence, I want you to re-examine your beliefs. What are the core beliefs you hold about yourself? For example, do you believe you are worthy? Do you believe you are special? Do you believe you are destined for greatness? Do you believe you are born for a unique purpose? Do you believe you are neither inferior nor superior to any human on Earth? Do you believe you are beautiful? Do you believe you are resilient? Do you believe you can do anything and everything you put your mind to doing and succeed?

Once you start operating based on your foundational beliefs and not on your sight/reality, there is a complete paradigm and mindset shift. This is where faith takes over... Your beliefs literally become the substance of the things you hope and dream for or have always hoped and dreamt for and concrete evidence of all that you have not yet seen or cannot physically see. In other words, they open the door and grant you full access to your ideal life—a truly fulfilling and purposeful life; the life you were born and destined to live. When your focus is on the core beliefs/convictions you hold, you begin to live and are driven by those core beliefs/convictions, your passions, and vision and not by your background, past and/or present reality; you defile the status quo and thrive beyond barriers and limitations, and can now see and access all that your physical eyes and sight are unable to see and perceive. You begin to follow/and lead with your heart and not your sight. This is the beginning of your breakthrough.

4) PASSION:

Let's imagine that your ring finger represents your passions. Hence, Ring finger = Passions (the code for your ring finger is your passions). It represents those things that you are most passionate about in life and enjoy doing—you find immense joy and fulfilment doing them.

From your current position you are unable to see your ring finger, and hence your passions. This finger is covered by your first three fingers. When we focus and rely on our sight to determine our current reality and shape our fundamental beliefs about us and our lives, it becomes difficult to look past our condition and present circumstances, especially the negative ones. As a result, our judgement of our life is based on our past and present life circumstances/ reality, making it hard for us to do the things we truly love and enjoy doing. Our past and present rip us of the life/things we are most passionate about and enjoy doing. We can't see past the former and, therefore, our beliefs are limited to our past and present and hinder us from moving forward into what is beyond our past and now...

This time, I want you to bend your first three fingers inwardly towards your palm and keep them down, holding the index and middle finger with your thumb. These fingers were previously obstructing your view of your ring finger, preventing you from seeing it. After bending these fingers, you are now capable of having access to your ring finger — which under normal circumstances you would be unable to see.

Once you have access to your passion and the things you enjoy doing, you begin enjoying life and living more authentically. You are no longer driven by your past failures and fears or present hardships and challenges but rather by your passions. It energises and motivates you to follow your heart and to be able to overcome future obstacles along the way. It provides you with fuel and the motivation to live a purposeful life that brings you ultimate fulfilment and joy. You are able to enjoy each day you are blessed with the gift of life, despite your shortcomings. You start living the life you once desired and loved... You start living your greatest heart's desires and dreams... You start seeing life differently and become more enthusiastic and passionate about life and what lies ahead of you each day... You become alive again irrespective of your past and current circumstances... This new energy, called passion, births in you a new drive and energy for living and enjoying life fully. It gives you the opportunity to see and focus on what you love and that brings you immense fulfilment and joy – your vision and life purpose. Passion makes you unstoppable in the face of challenges and propels you towards your vision/ purpose.

5) VISION:

Let's imagine that your pinky finger represents your vision. Hence, Pinky finger = Vision (the code for your pinky finger is your vision). It represents your purpose, your final destination here on Earth.

As you will notice, in your current position, your tiny finger/vision is completely out of sight and concealed. It is a function of the heart and not a function of the eyes, which is why you are unable to see it. Until you have successfully overcome all the barriers of your past, present, and limiting beliefs, and eventually are following your heart and your passions, you may not be able to see and move beyond them in order to get to your ultimate destination and fulfil your life purpose.

Consequently, in order to successfully arrive at your destiny and fulfil your vision, barriers need to be broken down. You must see outside of the box; you must also displace yourself and position yourself at a higher altitude and platform in order to be able to see your vision clearly. You must rise above limitations, barriers, and obstacles in cases where these cannot be broken. Hence, you must rise above your past, present, and limiting beliefs.

Vision could be defined as an internalised mental picture of an ideal life—a preferable future. It is also defined as an internalised mental picture of your purpose. It is your ability to break down barriers, and in cases where barriers cannot be broken it is your ability to see beyond barriers. It is your ability to see that which cannot be perceived or seen by the naked eyes/your sight. Vision is also the capacity to see that which others cannot see then plan and prepare for it. Vision is a function of the heart while sight is a function of the eyes. Vision is far greater than sight... It is more powerful than sight. Let your vision and not your sight drive you daily; only then will you be able to live a truly fulfilling and purposeful life—one that no eyes (including yours) have been able to see or even perceive yet.

Helen Keller, one of the greatest motivational speakers and transformational leaders of our time, who was blind, dumb, and deaf from the tender age of 18 months (following an illness), was once asked in an interview what could be the worst tragedy that could ever happen to someone other than being born blind. Her response was very simple yet profound. Smiling, she said/wrote on a sheet of paper, "The only thing worse than being blind is having sight but no vision."

In effect, she demonstrated that having eyes/sight wasn't indispensable for the fulfilment of her purpose; neither should being blind be an excuse to keep her from fulfilling her maximum potential/purpose. On the contrary, she travelled all over the world and impacted millions of lives through her inspirational speeches—even though she couldn't speak and was blind. She had an interpreter and could communicate by using a device and also by reading people's lips with her hands.

Here is someone we thought had limitations because she was blind and deaf, yet she understood that the real power that determines how successful and fulfilled you and I become in life is our vision, our ideal, that internalized mental picture of the preferred life that you want for yourself; it is that ideal future that you so much desire within and hope for—that eyes have not yet seen and ears have not yet heard about, but deep within your spirit you feel like you were born to live that life. She is a great example of someone who could have been labelled as disabled, yet she didn't let this impact her in any way. She spoke and transformed the lives of people like you and me who could see, speak, and hear. She was capable of transforming their lives, despite not being able to see, hear, or speak.

At this stage, I will borrow my 14-year-old daughter's quote. She is currently Liverpool's youngest best-selling author of three books and an entrepreneur. She wrote her first book, *Short Stories by Latoya Likambi*, when she was just seven years old and it was published when she turned ten. I was intrigued in one of her first interviews when she was asked about what message she had for children. She said, and I am quoting her, "Never let anyone put you down. You may have a disability, but you have so many special abilities and talents to do amazing things and talented things in this world. So never let anyone put you down." Wow!

That was from a ten-year-old girl; my own daughter saying it doesn't matter what the world calls disability, we all have special abilities and talents. Hence, we should never settle for anything beneath our vision and greatness. Your vision should be your ultimate focus and definition of your true self and purpose. Keep your eyes focused on your vision, the destination and finale! You are destined for greatness and success.

6) YOUR ATTITUDE

Now let's imagine that your palm represents your attitude. Hence, palm = Attitude (the code for your palm is your attitude). Just like your core beliefs, passions, and vision, you are aware of the fact that your palm is right there, keeping all your fingers connected, and you can also feel it, though you're unable to see it from your current position. It may be often neglected, especially as the focus is on our fingers—past, present, beliefs, passions, and vision. Nonetheless, all of the above could only make perfect sense and help us truly identify ourselves and appreciate our journey and life by having full ownership of all that we are and are becoming with each new day.

For example, your past might have been horrible and your present is horrible; oh yes! That's fine. So many people have gone through challenges as well in their lives and are currently going through some tough times. Yet, just like your beliefs (which shape your attitude), your attitude determines how you see, perceive, interpret and live your life. Your attitude is that which will take you from your past – a horrible past, which could have been a terrible mess – to a great future in which that mess of the past now serves as a powerful message of hope to the world and to all those who will encounter and go through a similar mess in their lives. Your attitude, then, has the power to transform a horrible/disgraceful past of oppression and depression into a prosperous and graceful future of hope and light in which you are transforming lives and represent a true testimonial, role model, and authority, leveraging your life experiences and demonstrating that victory is possible and always near no matter what. Of note, as inspiring and transformational as I am, I always say this to my students in my workshops and master classes, if I have someone with me who has gone through addiction and/or depression when I'm delivering a workshop to a group of addicted and/or depressed individuals, the simple truth is he/she stands a greater chance of inspiring and transforming the lives of these individuals than I do—simply because they can instantly relate to him/her more easily than they could to me... In addition, through this person, they can see hope and victory over their current addiction and/or depression. He is an authentic role model to them and testament to victory and success—which I may not be. This is why I always use role models as examples of success and victory in my teachings, so that my students may be able to relate to them and see victory/ hope in them.

As a result, it doesn't matter what you are going through in life right now or what you've gone through in the past; your attitude is critical and solely responsible for how you express yourself and live your current experience (which is inevitably shaped by the fundamental beliefs you hold about your past and present experiences). Furthermore, if you are reading this manuscript right now it unquestionably signifies that you are still alive and I want you to know that you are a victor not a victim. The fact that you are not dead yet signifies that you are an overcomer and have overcome/are overcoming the adversity you faced/are currently facing and your attitude will greatly determine your drive and your ability to conquer and succeed. Therefore, I want to lay emphasis on the fact that it is all about your attitude towards life, your life. Do you want to have an attitude of a victor or victim of your past/present? Do you want to transform your path, your past, your mess and everything negative that belongs to it into a brighter, hopeful, and prosperous future? It doesn't matter what your past and present look like. What is most important is where you are going to—your destination, your purpose. You never move forward by moving backwards or looking behind you ... you do so by moving forward and looking ahead of you where the journey leads. You never rise to your future by falling down or looking downwards ... you do so by looking up and lifting yourself upwards. You move on and focus on where you are heading to. Remember, your attitude defines the ultimate direction of movement.

Your attitude will literally make you become all that you were ever created to become or break you and leave you in mediocrity—below your maximum and true potential. Your attitude can either be a great and powerful bridge/ path that connects your past, present, beliefs, passions and vision and propels you forward into your future and life purpose or a massive wall and barrier that keeps your past, present, and beliefs, passions and vision/future forever disconnected, isolated, and separated, leaving you trapped in one phase of your life or the other and never giving you the opportunity to access your future/dreams and vision and fulfil your purpose. It rips you from the true joy of ever knowing all that you are and represent.

For this reason, a lion will forever remain the king of the jungle (animal kingdom), not because it is the most beautiful, tallest, heaviest, or even the strongest amongst all animals but simply because of its attitude. An invincible attitude. This is undoubtedly the reason why it is often said that an army of sheep led by a lion will always defeat an army of lions led by a sheep. The lion leader is capable of transforming the mindset of its sheep followers and gets them to believe, think, and to see themselves as lions/develop the invincible mindset/attitude of the lion leader and vice versa for the sheep leader.

Remember, as a man thinks so he is. Hence your thoughts and not the thoughts of others are responsible for shaping your life and predicting your life/destiny. Furthermore, people cannot access your thoughts or know your thoughts by merely looking at your past life and/or current reality. You might have developed a completely renewed mindset and, as a result, repented/transformed your thoughts about your past/ who you are... Hence, you have a renewed attitude.

CHAPTER TEN

CONCLUSION

> "Do not conform to the pattern of this world, but be transformed by the renewing of your mind. Then you will be able to test and approve what God's will is—his good, pleasing and perfect will."
>
> **Romans 12:2**

As you get to the final chapter of this manuscript, I urge you to forget/let go of whatever narrative/s and/or identity you have been told/given up to this date, especially if they are negative and disempowering. It is paramount that you never seek people's opinions on who you are. I will repeat. Never seek other people's opinion about your identity. Do not give them the right or permission to actually tell you who you are or tell your story and/or identify you. They have no clue of who you are. They have no clue of the greatness that's within you. They absolutely have no clue of the thoughts that go in between your mind. Some of them don't even know who they are... How then can they claim to know and/or tell you who you are? No one knows you (or should know you) any better than yourself... Just as no one thinks for you (should think for you) or knows your thoughts. You alone know your thoughts, just like your beliefs, which are so much engrained within you.

The truth is, even though you cannot always control what happens to you/ around you or what people think of you and/or how they see you or identify you, nevertheless you have the potential and power to control the way you respond to what happens to you/around you and what people do or say to you and about you. You also have the power to set the pace and determine your destiny, not people or circumstances and chance. You may not always be able to tell people to treat you in a certain way or not to call you certain names or undermine/label you before they do so. However, you have the potential and ability to choose and hold on to the way you want and desire to be treated, identified, and called and to respond the way you want to when they treat you in ways and manners that you disagree with and disapprove of.

Notwithstanding, the entire above can only be possible when you are truly secure and resolute in your true identity.

There is power in knowing your authentic identity. When you know who you are, people cannot label you. Or more appropriately, you cannot permit people to label you, put a stigma on you or determine who/what you are and/or you are not. People's opinions of you become irrelevant. This is because nobody knows you better than you know yourself or thinks the way you or your Creator thinks. Nobody is in your mind. Hence, how can you let me, society, some medical doctor, your teacher, or even your parents define you or determine who you are when they have no clue of the greatness that's within you? In addition, they have no clue of all that which is entrapped within your unique DNA. Tell me, how then could they tell who you are or will become?

Yes, you might have gone through some horrible things in your past. You might have been abused, you might have been a drug addict, and you might have been … you name it … yet, no one has the right to use these against you or to define you. Those were instances and circumstances in your life; those were moments of your life that were needed to prune and shape you into becoming all that you were created and destined to become. Just like gold has to go through a furnace, through hot fire to be purified and become pure, you needed to go through some of those challenges to bring out your best self and fulfil your life purpose.

There is only one narrative you should hold on to concerning your identity—and this originates from your source; from the originator of life, your life. You are born and destined for greatness … to have dominion over all things and circumstances... including all that you are going through right now or will ever go through in your lifetime! Go now and start living a life of purpose and greatness. Go on and unleash your authentic identity. I wish you a wonderful and thrilling journey to self-discovery and unlocking your unique purpose.

Maybe, growing up as a child, your parents might have put you down, abused you and told you that you were of no worth. Please! You need to take off that belief. That is what they believe about you; that is not necessarily what you should believe about yourself because, like I said earlier on, the ideal person to speak to about a product is its manufacturer. The ideal person to give the final say about you is your Creator, the Almighty God, and His final statement about you is that you are beautifully and wonderfully made; you are unique; you are destined for a purpose; you are a winner and not a loser; and it is in your Creator's best interest that you succeed because when you succeed, His brand succeeds and is trustworthy. You are created in His image. So, your success is fundamental.

I want to tell you that this is who you should be looking up to, not another man; not your spouse; not your friends; not your neighbours; not even your teachers; not your parents. They do not know who you are.

Reader's Authentic Identity

HOW HAS YOUR PAST SHAPED YOUR IDENTITY?

HOW DOES YOUR PRESENT SHAPE YOUR IDENTITY?

Reader's Authentic Identity

HOW DO YOUR CORE BELIEFS SHAPE YOUR IDENTITY?

HOW DO YOUR PASSIONS SHAPE YOUR IDENTITY?

_____
_____
_____
_____
_____
_____
_____
_____
_____
_____
_____
_____
_____
_____
_____
_____

_____
_____
_____
_____
_____

Reader's Authentic Identity

HOW DOES YOUR VISION/ PURPOSE SHAPE YOUR IDENTITY?

HOW DOES YOUR ATTITUDE SHAPE YOUR IDENTITY?

_____

_____

_____

_____

_____

_____

_____

_____

_____

_____

_____

_____

_____

_____

_____

_____

_____

_____

_____

_____

AUTHOR'S BIOGRAPHY

Dr Sylvia Forchap-Likambi is a visionary, multi-award-winning leading empowerment and transformation authority, transformational speaker/coach, and four-time international best-selling author, specialising in the delivery of very high-quality/cutting-edge empowerment and revolutionary leadership and transformation programs. She is the founder and CEO of "Behaviour Changed", the award-winning community interest company, Voice of Nations, and founder/global chair of The Global Visionary Women Network and global CEO/consultant of Dr Sylvia Likambi International/Dr Sylvia Likambi International Health & Well-being Clinic.

Over the years, she has coached, empowered, inspired, and positively impacted/transformed over one and a half million lives globally, including thousands of female entrepreneurs, and relentlessly empowered many to come out of addictions and depression and get into training, volunteering, employment/self-employment, and even leadership roles and also offered them several such opportunities through her organisations.

She has featured on several national and international radio and TV stations and been guest/keynote speaker to several national and international audiences, ranging from community groups to universities. For more information about Dr Sylvia Forchap-Likambi and her work, or to invite her for an interview or to deliver some of her cutting-edge transformational programs and talks to your team or company, please contact her using the details below:

Email: forchaps@drsylvialikambi.com

Tel: +44 (0) 7539 216072

- www.voiceofnations.org.uk
- www.globalvisionarywomennetwork.org
- www.drsylvialikambi.com
- www.likambiglobalpublishing.com

Published by Likambi Global Publishing Ltd.

We are a Dynamic Family-Led Cutting-Edge Global Publisher set up to simplify and enhance your writing and publishing experience and unique journey to becoming a renowned and confident author.

Whether you are an adult or a child, we have a bespoke package and special team that is devoted to working with you throughout your writing and publishing journey with us!

All of our consultants and coaches/ mentors are best-selling authors with years of hands-on experience and a wealth of knowledge uniquely tailored to meet your individual needs!

Our goal is to provide you with the ultimate writing and publishing experience required to share your unique message and voice as an author with the world and strive to greater heights and platforms!

Publications are done three times a year, in January, June and November.

All manuscripts must be received at least 90 days prior to publication dates.

Likambi Global Publishing Contact Details

Website:
www.likambiglobalpublishing.com

Email:
enquiries@likambiglobalpublishing.com

Address:
208a Picton Road, Liverpool, L15 4LL
United Kingdom

www.ingramcontent.com/pod-product-compliance
Lightning Source LLC
Chambersburg PA
CBHW050730030426

42336CB00012B/1492